KILL CRAZY GANG:

THE CRIMES OF THE LEWIS-JONES GANG

JEFFERY S. KING

ISBN: 0615660428
ISBN 13: 9780615660424

The Frank Manley Publishing Company, 2013.
Washington, D.C.

Library of Congress Control Number: 2012952799
CreateSpace Independent Publishing Platform
North Charleston, South Carolina

ACKNOWLEDGMENTS

Retired Colorado Springs, Colorado, police investigator and historian Dwight Haverkorn, who has spent many years researching the history of the Colorado Springs police department, including the Lewis-Jones gang, was of great help to me. Rene Barratt did the cover design and Monica Ramsey did the proofreading and the index. I also want to thank crime historian David Murray of Inverness, Scotland, Thomas Man of the Library of Congress, Roy Young of the Wild West History Association, and the staff of the Manuscript Division of the Library of Congress, who helped me with the Sherrill-Lewis- Jones gang file in the Pinkerton Detective Agency manuscript. The photos in this book are from the Sherrill- Lewis-Jones gang file Ingrid Hidalgo helped me with my computer.

CONTENTS:

PART ONE

PART TWO

INTRODUCTION

The period from 1866 to 1936 was the golden age of crime. Criminals could become celebrities or be considered Robin Hoods and survive for years. Jesse James, the Dalton boys, Billy the Kid, and Butch Cassidy and the Sundance Kid were some of these bandits.

But popular interest in criminals shows a gap in the 1910s, between the horseback outlaws of earlier years and the automobile bandits of the 1920s and 1930s, such as John Dillinger, Baby Face Nelson, Pretty Boy Floyd, Bonnie and Clyde, and the Barker/Karpis Gang. One of the most violent gangs of those years was the Lewis-Jones gang, which used the emerging automobile culture to steal, kill, and outwit lawmen, as the following chapters describe.

THE GANG

The Lewis-Jones gang of the 1910s came out of Oklahoma, home of such notorious outlaws as the Doolins, Henry Starr, and "Pretty Boy" Floyd. One of the first gangs to use the automobile, it was the forerunner of the major bandit gangs of the 1930s.[1]

According to an article in *Real Detective*:

> *But in the lurid crime annals of the Southwest, the crimson records of the Lewis Boys easily over matched all the rest. Train robbers, bank looters, prison breakers, wanton murderers, they are said to have killed twenty-one police officers and maimed a dozen more before the law finally wiped them out. Their exploits cause the raids of the John Dillingers and the Clyde Barrows to seem by comparison, little more than Sunday School picnics.*[2]

US Post Office Inspector W. N. Hughes, who was involved in the hunt for the gang, stated:

> *They talk about Jesse James and his gang! They couldn't hold a candle for this outfit. These men were the worst the West has ever seen. It is doubtful whether the country will ever see the like of them. They were fearless and were experts with the rifle and the revolver, and on the top of all this they had no more regard for human life than they had for a street dog.*[3]

The *Parsons* (Kansas) *Daily Republican* called the gang, "The most desperate train robbery gang in the history of the southwest."[4] The gang was truly "kill-crazy." That term was sometimes used by lawmen, criminals and newspaper reporters. For example, in 1933 criminal Ed Shouse of the Dillinger gang, said "They are kill-crazy, and that is why I left them."[5]

The Lewis-Jones gang was active at the same time as the Poe-Hart gang in Oklahoma (1916–17), the Ashley gang of Florida (1915–21), and Henry Starr of Oklahoma (1891–1921).[6]

THE AUTOMOBILE

In 1886 Carl Benz had patented the world's first practical motorcar. Between 1900 and 1920, motor-vehicle registrations multiplied a thousandfold, from eight thousand to eight million. On

October 1, 1908, the first cheap Ford Model T—selling for $850—appeared. Built on an assembly line, the Model T took the automobile out of the tinkerer's garage and into everyone's garage. In 1913 Gulf opened the first drive-in gas station in Pittsburgh.

Automobiles greatly increased the mobility of criminals in the early 1900s. The first stolen car in the United States was in St. Louis in 1905.[7] That year, the *New York Times* began to record crimes in which cars were involved, especially burglaries,[8] and the silent film *The Gentlemen Highwaymen* showed criminals making getaways in cars.[9]

On August 13, 1909, two bandits with shotguns held up the Santa Clara Valley Bank at Santa Clara, California, grabbing about $7,000 and escaping in a hired car. Although this was one of the first bank robberies in which the criminals used automobiles, the thieves were caught seven miles from town by a posse on horseback.[10]

By 1911 crimes involving automobiles had become a serious problem. On December 21, 1911, a gang led by Jules Joseph Bonnot, the first European to use a car in a bank robbery, stole $333,500 in paper and gold from the Saint-Ouen branch of the Societe General Bank in Paris. Bonnot killed himself on April 29, 1912, when surrounded by police, who also killed an accomplice. His crimes were well publicized in America.[11] During the 1910s many bank robberies were still committed on horseback, but by the 1920s almost all criminals used cars in their heists.[12] The *Los Angeles Times* noted in 1916:

> *The automobile gives the criminal a start over the law that is almost a prohibitive handicap. An auto bandit can commit a crime, escape and be miles away before the police learn of it. Such a condition lends bravery and audacity to the most timid criminal…Crime waves such as we are now experiencing are due entirely to the wonderful speed of the automobile. Present laws are not adequate, as they were drawn at a time when men traveled on horseback.*[13]

The transition for turn-of-the-century criminals was not as easy as it would seem. The roads were very poor, often made of dirt. They became very muddy. There were only a few gasoline stations, so police could easily keep a close watch on them. With the passage of the National Road Act of 1916 things greatly improved. More and better roads were built.[14]

THE LAWMEN

Lawmen tried, mostly unsuccessfully, to keep up with the criminal use of the automobile. The first police car was a Stanley Steamer used by the Boston Police Department in 1902. However, the police were limited by county and state lines, and criminals had faster cars.[15]

The main national police organization of the time was the Pinkerton National Detective Agency, a pioneer in law enforcement. For example, Pinkerton developed the first rogues' gallery. Founded in 1850 by Allan Pinkerton, the agency pursued notorious outlaws such as the James-Younger gang and Butch Cassidy and the Sundance Kid. Pinkerton had discovered a plot to kill President Lincoln when Lincoln was on his way to Washington for his first inauguration. Pinkerton fooled the plotters by having the president take an earlier train. Allan Pinkerton died in 1884; his sons William and Robert continued to run the firm. [16]

The Federal Bureau of Investigation, founded in 1908 and at the time known as the Bureau of Investigation in the US Department of Justice, had almost no involvement in local crime. It was then considered to be a very minor law-enforcement agency. Not until 1919, with the passage of the Dyer Act, did it gain the authority to investigate the interstate transportation of stolen cars—a major expansion of federal police authority, for many criminals drove stolen cars across state lines. For example, many years later the FBI was able to go after John Dillinger on the basis that he had driven a stolen car across state lines.[17]

The Postal Inspection Service of the United States Post Office was also active in the hunt for the Lewis-Jones gang after they robbed the mails during a train robbery. Its jurisdiction was defined as "crimes that may adversely affect or fraudulently use the U.S. Mail, the postal system or postal employees." It was one of the oldest law-enforcement agencies in the United States, having begun in 1772 when colonial Postmaster General Benjamin Franklin appointed a "surveyor" to audit and regulate the mails.[18]

PART ONE

CHAPTER 1:

A FAMILY OF OUTLAWS

Elsworth and Martha Lewis, who were married in 1885, were the parents of the Lewis outlaws. Elsworth was a lawman by trade and also worked as a butcher and farmer.[1] He was a cruel, hot-tempered, half-Cherokee man who often beat his wife and children and was said to have killed two men.[2] Martha was from the Cherokee Nation and could not read or write. She sometimes worked as a ballyhoo or "spieler" at street fairs.[3] They had six children: Stella (born in December 1886 in Illinois), Oscar Lee (born in August 1888 in Kansas), Roy Joe (born on August 19, 1890, in Kansas), Frank (born in July 1892 in Indian Territory), Ora (born on February 14, 1897, in Illinois), and Eva (born on January 27, 1899, in Indian Territory).[4]

Frank "Jumbo" Lewis looked older than he was. He was five feet nine inches, weighed 250 pounds, and had hazel eyes and coarse, dark hair, with a round, full face. There was a blurred tattoo of a nude woman and crossed cannons on his left forearm. He had a large abdomen, and wore a low belt and a size-seventeen shirt.[5]

Ora Otis, alias "Mutt," Lewis was also five feet nine inches tall and weighed about 160 pounds, with a medium build, dark-brown hair, blue eyes, and dark complexion. He usually wore a glove to hide a raised scar on the back of his left hand.

Oscar Lee was five feet seven inches tall, weighed about 150 pounds, and had brown hair, blue eyes, and a medium complexion.[6]

Roy Joe was the tallest at five feet ten and a quarter inches tall. He weighed 134 pounds, and had black hair and blue eyes, with a dark complexion. He had worked as a machinist.[7]

The beautiful Eva was five feet five inches tall. She weighed 105 pounds, and had a slender build, medium brown hair, blue eyes, and a medium complexion.[8]

Sometime after the turn of the century, the Lewis family moved to Galena, Kansas, where Elsworth was a night policeman. Roy falsely claimed his father had been the police chief of Galena.[9] Galena had been established in southeast Kansas in 1877 when huge deposits of lead were found. Overnight the boomtown had a population of almost ten thousand, and by 1898 the town had almost thirty thousand people. Innumerable saloons and gambling halls attracted murderers, outlaws, and gamblers. Some miners were killed for their money. Galena had 265 producing mines, 2 banks, 36 grocers, and more than 48 other retail stores.[10]

The family next moved to Junction City, Kansas, where Elsworth was again a policeman.[11] Located at the confluence of the Republican and Smoky Hill Rivers, the town, incorporated in 1859, was a trading center for Fort Riley in northeast Kansas and had a great future as a wholesale and trans-shipping point. Military roads from Fort Riley to western outposts linked the town with the Santa Fe Trail and Mormon Trail. The Smoky Hill Trail passed through Junction City. Within ten years, it had become a thriving community.[12]

Near the end of his life, Frank Lewis declared:

> *To my father goes the blame for me being here today. He taught me the ways of crime and if I ever had the opportunity again to meet him would surely kill him.*
>
> *When I was only 14 years of age and when my father was a policeman at Junction City, Kansas, he took me with him to assist in robbing places. Many times he held me up to transoms thru which I climbed and unlocked the doors so he could make a haul. During all this time, my mother thought I was leading a good life and I don't believe that she knows that I have any connection with crime.*
>
> *Yes, I realized when it was too late that I was traveling the wrong road.*[13]

Frank was the first of the Lewis siblings to suggest they start a criminal career, when Roy was about sixteen. According to Roy, Frank and Ora had always been bad. As he put it, "Frank was bad and Ora was hell. Ora was always practicing with a gun, and Frank was some shooter."[14]

His mother had thought Ora was of "unsound mind" since he was four years old.[15] "When Ora was four years old we were living in Kansas City. One day he wandered from home and was lost eleven days. When he returned he had a gash over his right eye. He never has been normal since."[16]

Ora later said, "I got my start in Chetopa, Kansas, when I was 8 years old. I stole a tricycle from a kid, and I've been stealing ever since. Some record, eh?"

His fourteen-year-old niece Gertrude Landon, daughter of Stella Lewis, later told reporters:

He used to beat me when I was 4 years old. This was when I wouldn't play with toys with him. Even when he was 19 years old Ora was always was wanting to play with blocks."

Many times on pay day nights he wouldn't give me a nickel for candy, unless I would help him build a house, something out of blocks. He became angry if I refused to play with him, and wouldn't speak with me for days.[17]

Finally Martha and the family left Elsworth and moved to Ponca City, Oklahoma, where Martha had a homestead. She divorced Elsworth.[18] Ponca City, located in the north-central part of the state, eighteen miles south of the Kansas border, was founded in 1893 as New Ponca following the Cherokee Outlet land run. The site for the city was chosen because it was near the Arkansas River and a freshwater spring.[19]

THE CHEROKEE OUTLET

The Cherokee Outlet was land in Indian Territory (now Oklahoma) set aside for Cherokees from North Carolina, Tennessee, and Georgia when they were driven from these states. The Treaty of New Echota, signed in 1835, set up a perpetual outlet in the West. Mostly unused by whites until after the Civil War, the land enabled Indians to hunt buffalo unmolested. Much of the land was given to other tribes. In the 1880s the Cherokees let cattlemen use their land for a fee.

Immigrants and others were hungry for the land in the Cherokee Outlet. Finally Congress offered the Cherokees $8.3 million for their territory in 1893, which the tribe accepted. On September 16, 1893, there was the greatest land rush in American history when the vast grassland was opened for white settlement. At noon that day, more than a hundred thousand people along four hundred miles of border waited for the pistol shots that started the land rush. The prize was a quarter section or a town lot to every eligible settler who staked a claim. People arrived by city cabs, bicycles, covered wagons, buggies, ox teams, race horses, and special railroad train cars. Some even walked. By nightfall the Cherokee Outlet consisted of numerous townsites and homesites.[20]

CHAPTER 2:

"BELIEVE ME WE DID SOME STEALING"

By 1912 Martha had remarried, to a successful, mild-mannered photographer named John Bubb. They were then living in Tulsa. Frank, Ora, and Roy worked as truck drivers, taking baggage to and from the Tulsa depot. Tall, dark, and handsome, Roy was the silent type; he had driven the first truck in the neighborhood. He took a job driving a baggage truck in Kansas City and was involved in an accident in which a passenger was killed. Greatly upset, Roy returned to Tulsa. The restless Ora often caught a freight train to nearby towns. After a few days he would return home, dirty and hungry. Oscar was a good boy who stayed at home helping the family by taking odd jobs, as did Stella. Eva wanted to go into show business and studied dancing and singing.[1] Frank, a psychopath who was popular with women, had gunshot wounds in his breast and a stiff right arm. Usually Frank, who posed as an oil or stock man, wore black button shoes with bulldog toes. He constantly smoked cigars.[2]

Martha was suspicious of her children. Once she asked Ora and Frank where they got so much money and why they always had the curtains of their automobile drawn. The brothers told her they took women across the river on joy rides and the women did not want to be seen.[3]

Around 1912 only a few people drove automobiles, but the four Lewis boys loved to fool around with cars. In Carthage, Missouri, Ora stole a beautiful car and headed for Tulsa. On the way it broke down, and he was arrested. Placed in the Webb City, Missouri, jail, his photo was taken, and he gave his real name. He subsequently escaped by making a hole in the brick jail wall.

The Tulsa police often visited the Lewis home looking for Ora, so the brothers left for Kansas City, Missouri, where for two years Frank drove a truck. The brothers mostly robbed grocery stores and mercantile establishments in small Kansas towns. Once they stole horse collars from a harness shop in Neosho, Missouri. They also committed burglaries and stole cars in Missouri and Kansas, as well as Tulsa.

In 1912 a night watchman at a Kansas City, Kansas, wholesale house shot Frank nine times in the chest. Ora severely beat the watchman, placed Frank in their car, and headed for Tulsa. Miraculously Frank recovered in a few weeks.[4]

Frank then went to Wichita, Kansas, and later claimed he hauled whiskey to Oklahoma and other states for about a year for $200 a week.[5] The Lewis boys once robbed a whiskey runner and escaped from the sheriff in a high-powered car.[6] Frank later said, "I had everything a man could want in this world with the exception of one thing and that was happiness."[7]

The Lewis boys, except for Roy, were all arrested in 1913. Ora was arrested in Joplin, Missouri, for stealing seventeen cars; all but one were recovered. He developed smallpox while at the county jail and was taken to the pest house, from which he escaped while still suffering from the disease. Ora's wife, who lived in Joplin, sued him for divorce. Frank was arrested in St. Louis, charged with stealing a car from his employer in Rich Hill, Missouri, and was sent back there. Apparently he was soon released. About the same time, Oscar was captured after a gunfight with officers, sent back to Tulsa and charged with rolling a Tulsa pawnshop. Twenty revolvers were found in his suitcase, but he was soon released for lack of evidence.[8] Oscar was very much against killing anyone, but Frank and Ora told him they would "bump off" any cop who got in their way.

It is unknown what the Lewis brothers did in 1914.

Roy split from the gang so he could "live decent." The happiest time of his life was when he lived with his wife in Fort Smith, Arkansas, working as a teamster. In early 1915, Frank and Ora visited Roy in Fort Smith and told him he was "a dern fool" for being an honest man. He agreed and later said, "Believe me we did some stealing."[9]

PROHIBITION

In 1880 Kansas voters passed a ballot proposal for a constitutional amendment that made illegal the manufacture and sale of intoxicating liquors. Kansas was the second state, after Maine, to enact laws prohibiting alcohol. Despite the constitutional amendment, many saloons and breweries continued to operate. Kansas law allowed citizens to have alcohol for "medicinal purposes." Beginning in 1899, Carrie Nation, a leader in the temperance movement, smashed many saloons operating illegally in Kansas. Ironically her husband drank himself to death.[10] On September 17, 1907, prohibition became part of Oklahoma's constitution. However, enforcement of prohibition in Oklahoma was very weak.[11]

CHAPTER 3:

MURDER IN A SHOE STORE

About a half hour past midnight on May 20, 1915, Ora, Roy, and Frank Lewis entered the A. E. Bump Shoe Store in Wichita through a rear door and twirled the dials on the store safe. A couple going to bed had seen from their apartment window the three men breaking into the store, and they called the police. Meanwhile, Patrolman Al Harrell, who was passing by, saw through the plate-glass store window the shadows of two men near the safe. After finding the front door locked, Harrell went around to the rear door. Discovering it was open, he stayed there about ten minutes before he left to turn in the call at a livery stable.

Immediately, Captain Frank Griswold started for the scene. On the way he picked up a special officer named Cruse, and they met Harrell at the shoe store's rear door. The captain sent Cruse around to guard the front door. They were not sure if the robbers had left while Harrell had been away. With Harrell going in first, they entered the open rear door at one a. m... Griswold turned on the flashlight he held in his left hand. A noise came from the center of the store near the cash register. In the darkness, Griswold hurried toward it. They heard another noise in the washroom in the back.[1]

"Come on out of there and have your hands up when you come," shouted Griswold. There was no answer.[2]

"Come out of there or I'll shoot," Harrell yelled.[3]

From the shadows, the Lewis boys came out firing at the light, with the officers returning the fire. A robber near the cash register shot the captain in his side, the .32-caliber bullet entering his left breast between the second and third ribs and going downward through both lungs near the heart, lodging under the right shoulder blade. Another bullet struck the back of his head and entered his brain.[4]

"They have got me. I am done for, Al," Griswold exclaimed and then fell dead.[5]

A bone in Harrell's right arm was shattered. It was possible that when Griswold was shot, he fired aimlessly and may have hit Harrell's arm. When Cruse looked through the front window, a bullet struck it, and he ducked back. Harrell escaped from the store by kicking out the glass in the front door and falling out. Cruse helped him get out of the line of fire.[6]

"The Captain is in there and down," Harrell said.[7]

Harrell was taken to the Wichita hospital, where an operation was performed to cut out the splintered section of the patrolman's bone; afterward his right arm was two inches shorter than his left arm.

The gang escaped through the rear door, although this was not known for fully a half hour after the gunfight. One of the robbers was believed to be wounded. No one had guarded the back door for ten minutes. People living in rooms above saw three men run through an alley after the shooting.

Two more officers reached the scene about fifteen minutes after the gun battle. One guarded the backdoor, while the other stayed at the front entrance. Since the interior of the store was completely dark and the street was bright, and since it was thought the robbers were still inside, the officers hesitated to enter. More policemen, including officer J. William Murrell, and a crowd of about fifty citizens soon arrived on the scene.[8]

"If the captain is in there, someone ought to go into him. By God. I'm going in. Come on. I'll lead the way," Murrell shouted.[9]

When Murrell and two other officers entered the store and turned on the lights, the crowd flocked in. Mr. Bump, owner of the store, was called to the scene. He found that the robbers had taken only twenty-five dollars in small change from under a counter near the cash drawer. Chief of Police O. K. Stewart joined the squad, marshaled the entire police force, and gave orders to arrest every suspicious person in the city. Officer Harrell told the police chief he believed one of the robbers had been wounded. The local sheriff, members of the Anti-Horse Thief Association, and police in nearby cities joined the manhunt.

The fifty-six-year-old Griswold left a widow and four children. A standing reward of $300 was offered by the Sedgwick County commissioners for the arrest and conviction of the slayers.[10] The following Sunday evening at St. Paul's Church, Dr. J. W. Somerville said, "They [the policemen] are just as heroic as any soldier that ever went to the battlefield."[11]

Planning to go to Mexico, the killers fled to Long Beach, California, until they read a newspaper account that the border was being watched for them.[12]

CHAPTER 4:

"HE'S HARD OF HEARING, DON'T SHOOT"

In July 1915 the Lewis family set up headquarters in St. Louis, where they purchased an expensive house next to the mayor's home. Later they moved to another house in that city. For several months the gang was very successful robbing stores in the Midwest. Eva, known as one of the best and most attractive female singers and dancers in the St. Louis region, was very popular at local nightclubs.

Because of World War I, prices were high for copper, lead, and zinc, so throughout Missouri the gang stripped poles of high-tension wires worth more than a quarter million dollars.[1] While stealing wire, Roy had several escapes from death. Near Continental, Missouri, while he was cutting trolley wire, one end of it burned his exposed leg. Another time, when the Lewis boys were stealing thirty-five hundred pounds of trolley wire near Staunton, Illinois, the wire fell across a rail. The resulting big blue flare could be seen for miles. Usually the criminals received between eighteen and twenty cents a pound, but sometimes they sold the stolen wire for as little as eight cents a pound.[2]

Ora would often sell stolen goods to fences. Sometimes the gang met the fences on the road and transferred the stolen goods from their automobiles to the fence's car. One time a fence bought automobile tire inner tubes from them, and the gang later robbed the fence's store and took all the inner tubes he had. A few days later, when they sold the fence his own automobile parts, the fence told them about the burglary.

Once the Lewis brothers met a peddler with his pack on the road. They pretended to be policemen and asked for his license, which he did not have. The criminals forced him to go with them. Finally the peddler accused them of being robbers and threw his wallet from the vehicle. The thugs backed their car up and found the wallet with $39.50 in it. The peddler and his backpack were thrown out of the vehicle. "That peddler's got no kick comin'," Roy later remarked. "He lost $39, but he got a joy ride worth a hundred dollars."[3]

At nine at night on Saturday, October 9, 1915, two masked members of the Lewis boys' gang, with caps pulled low and handkerchiefs over their faces, crouched as they walked into the Sutton Grocery in Wichita. They pointed guns at customer Grover Younkin and clerk William Routon and drove them back toward the rear where William Sutton, the grocer, and his son-in-law, Thomas A. Wilhite, were standing behind a meat counter.[4] "Stick 'em up and get down where you can't be seen from the street," ordered one of the gunmen.[5]

Younkin and the clerk obeyed. At that moment, John Koontz entered and was made to go behind the counter and kneel. The slightly deaf grocer was slow to kneel when commanded. The order was loudly repeated. Thinking the bandits wanted money, Sutton moved his right hand toward his hip pocket where there was a wallet containing money and checks.[6] "He's hard of hearing. Don't shoot," both Wilhite and Koontz yelled.[7]

As they spoke, the bandits fired. The grocer, killed instantly by a bullet entering through one eye, fell at the passageway between the meat counters. As one robber grabbed fifty dollars from a cash register on a meat counter, Wilhite rushed toward the dead man; he fell after being shot in the neck, right hand, and left side. The other bandit then went to the door and looked out, while his partner bent down to the dead grocer's body and took his wallet containing a total of $76.21: $15 in cash and the rest in checks. "Come on," yelled the robber at the door.[8]

"Is there anyone coming?" asked the other.

"Aw, come on."[9]

They ran out of the store, dropped the wallet without removing the money, and escaped in an auto; the wallet was found Sunday morning. At first it was believed Wilhite was dying, but he later recovered. A three-hundred-dollar reward was offered by the Sedgwick County commissioners for the capture of the murderers.[10]

Later that October, just before daylight one day, the Lewis boys used a hammer to break a window in a Topeka, Kansas, jewelry store and grabbed what they wanted. Ora was arrested in St. Louis a few days later when he was found in possession of some of the stolen jewelry; he was released because of a lack of evidence. During the next few months, the gang stole cars and wire and committed burglaries.[11]

In January 1916, the Lewis boys stole a truck of clothes belonging to J. D. Wooster Lambert, a rich young man from St. Louis, at a freight depot at Clayton, Missouri.[12]

The next month, Frank, Roy, and Ora drove to Pacific, Missouri, where they got stuck in the mud and had a flat tire. A wheel came off when the gangsters reached St. Louis at eight o'clock in the evening. As they waited to catch a streetcar, a police officer suddenly came up to them. The Lewis boys ran until they jumped into a car occupied by Mr. and Mrs. E. G. Beach and their chauffeur in front of the St. Regis apartments. Heading directly toward them, the officer pulled his revolver and fired. Frank returned the gunfire as the trio jumped into the vehicle. Ora's gun discharged by accident, the bullet going into the cushions.[13]

"Drive on quick," Ora ordered.

"What will we do, stick them up?" Ora asked.

"No, they have treated us all right," Roy responded.

"I don't think it would be a good idea to stick them up," Frank said as he forced the chauffeur to drive like hell and make sharp turns.

"That is enough," Frank said finally and ordered the chauffeur out.[14]

When the chauffeur didn't get out, the gangster took the wheel, slowing down to about ten miles an hour, and again told the chauffeur to get out. When the chauffeur asked the gangster to stop, Frank pushed him from the running board. Sitting in the back with Ora, the couple were also forced to get out. Frank drove away and later abandoned the vehicle.[15]

In March Frank drove alone past a hospital where he saw through a window that a house on the hospital grounds had a lot of hams inside, evidently belonging to the hospital. That same night the three brothers drove there and stole about twelve hams. They did not sell any of the hams, intending to use them for their personal use. Frank told his family he had gotten them cheap.[16]

On the afternoon of March 21, 1916, Roy entered the St. Louis home of Mrs. William Anderson and took two diamond rings, valued at $164 and $125 each, plus a half dollar. Meeting the burglar in the hall of her house, Mrs. Anderson asked him what he was doing there. Roy answered that he was looking for somebody and the doorbell had not rung. Then he left.[17]

CHAPTER 5:

"DON'T DO THAT, DON'T DO THAT"

Because of many recent gas-station robberies, St. Louis motorcycle squad patrolman John F. McKenna and other city officers paid close attention to all gas stations. On the morning of April 7, 1916, McKenna saw two men in a mud-spattered Ford circle two stations and then stop at a nearby garage used by the Lewis boys.[1]

The night before, the gang had stolen eight hundred pounds of copper wire from a streetcar barn in Hannibal, Missouri. They had also cut down and stolen about twelve hundred pounds of copper trolley wire a couple of miles from Mexico, Missouri. As they were going back to St. Louis, they stole a bicycle from the front lawn of a house in Mexico.

When Ora drove up to the garage in the St. Louis alley, Roy leaped out and opened the garage door. The officer came up to Ora, who remained in the car.[2]

"Where does that machine belong?" asked McKenna.[3]

"Right here," Ora replied.[4]

After looking into the vehicle and seeing copper wire, McKenna stepped back and drew his gun.[5]

"You come on, I want you," he said.[6]

The officer also ordered Roy to get out of the garage.[7]

Nearby, in a stolen Hudson, Frank and Oscar saw their brothers being arrested and backed up.

McKenna searched Roy and Ora and found a loaded revolver on Roy. Unfortunately, he did not realize Ora also had a gun, and he took the criminals to the nearby Motor Gasoline Company gas station. It was 7:50 a.m.. The officer ordered the attendant to, "Call the police station."

McKenna gave permission for Ora to get a drink of water at the far end of the station. After ostensibly getting the drink, Ora suddenly whirled around with a revolver in his hand and killed McKenna with a shot to his head while the attendant was on the telephone.[8] The gangster later claimed he had only intended to stick him up, but that the gun accidentally discharged and McKenna was killed.[9]

A black janitor named John Walker was in the alley near the station when he saw the arrest and heard the shot. The bandits ran past him as Ora was stuffing a revolver in his pocket.[10] "Lord have mercy," he said, "somebody's been shot."[11]

The two bandits ran to their car, jumped in, and fled rapidly away. Clarence J. Conway, a truck driver who had heard the shot, followed them but soon lost them.[12] Meanwhile, the gas station attendant gave the police a good description of the killers and their car.

Frank and Oscar drove past the station and heard McKenna being shot.[13]

"Come on, let's go up and get that cop," Frank said.[14]

"No, I'm not going to be in on anything like that in broad daylight, you fool," his brother responded.

"Get out of the car; I'll do it myself," Frank ordered.

As Frank continued driving, Oscar jumped out and took a streetcar to the Lewis family house, taking about twenty minutes to get home; his brothers drove there.[15]

"I bet the Chief heard the shot [on the phone at the gas station]," Ora remarked after he was in the garage of his home.[16]

Oscar came into the garage and asked, "Did you kill him?"[17]

"I think I did," replied Ora.[18]

Not willing to accept a murder charge, Oscar went upstairs to kiss his mother good-bye, left the house and the gang, and disappeared.[19]

At 8:08 a.m., Patrolman William A. Dillon telephoned his police station and was told to be on the lookout for the murderers and their car. A few minutes later, he saw Roy and Ora inside a Ford that matched the description he was given entering a garage in an alley. At the same time, Frank drove the stolen Hudson into the alley at the other end and also entered the garage.

As Dillon ran up the alley and into the garage, he was grabbed by the thugs. Two boys on their way to school at 8:15 a.m. watched Dillon struggle with Roy in the garage and saw something "shiny"—a knife or gun—in Ora's hands. Actually it was a small hunting ax.[20] "Don't do that, don't do that," Dillon screamed.[21]

Berserk, Ora closed the garage door and hit the officer on the head and body thirteen times with the hunting ax. Blood spattered on the garage door, floor, and cars.[22]

"Jesus Christ, you have killed him," Roy said.

"What should we do with him?" Frank asked.

"We got him," Ora said. "Keep still and everything will be all right. We got to take this stuff [the bloody hatchet and shovel] out. It's got blood on it."[23]

After wrapping Dillon's body in a blanket, Frank and Ora drove away in the two cars. About eight thirty that morning, a man reported to the police that he saw someone transferring a bundle from a Ford to a Hudson, then get into the Hudson and abandon the Ford.[24] The gangsters stopped at a gas station and brought five gallons of gasoline.[25] Going deep into St. Louis County, the brothers buried Dillon's body in a culvert, threw out a torn police cap and a bloody floor mat from the car, and then drove at thirty miles an hour several miles toward St. Louis.[26]

"What will we do with this copper wire?" Frank asked.

"I don't know. We better leave it in the car and get rid of the car," Ora replied.

Just before reaching St. Louis, the gangsters came across a junkman with a wagon. They stopped him, and he agreed to buy the copper wire. As they started to load it onto the wagon, a farmer and another man came up, noticed blood on the running board, and looked at the license plate.

"What are you looking at," Frank asked and threatened to knock the farmer's brains out if he did not get away. When the two men walked away, the bandits stopped putting the rest of the copper wire in the wagon. They got $1.50 for about fifty pounds from the junkman.

"Let's get rid of this car," Ora said.

"Where will we take it?" Frank asked.

"Take it close to a streetcar line," Ora replied.

After the gangsters abandoned the Hudson, Ora rode home on the bicycle, while

Frank jumped onto a streetcar.[27]

At 9:50 a.m., the twenty-nine-year-old McKenna died at the city hospital without gaining consciousness. He had formerly been a police telephone operator and was a motorcycle policeman for about five years. Two of his relatives were also members of the police force. He left behind a wife.

When Dillon did not appear at his relief post at one o'clock, other policemen noticed his absence. A woman had come into the station and reported that she had seen a policeman go into a garage, but not come out.

The abandoned Hudson was found an hour later. On the left-hand door was blood-coagulated matter, possibly mixed with brain tissue. In it were strands of black hair mixed with gray like Dillon's, two hundred pounds of stolen copper wire, and a mud-covered police-coat brass button. At three in the afternoon, a bloodhound started from the Hudson and took a trail to a railroad crossing, where a watchman said he had seen two men board a westbound freight train earlier in the afternoon.[28]

About this time, Roy and Ora returned to the Lewis house.[29] Frank found another junk dealer and sold him copper wire.[30] Five hours later, Frank and his wife, Jennie, and Ora and Roy ate supper. Afterward, Ora drove Frank and his wife to Frank's place and stayed there with them.[31]

Numerous arrests were made that night, including Lewis family members John and Martha Bubb, Stella Landon, and Eva. The young Gertrude Landon was also questioned.

The next day a police squad came to the Lewis house and found Roy in bed. Roy, the nicest of the Lewis boys and the last to go into crime, was the first to be arrested. He blamed Frank and Ora for beating Dillon to death and denied that he took any part in the murder. Bloodstains were discovered in the garage.[32]

Eva called Frank's place. "Beat it Ora, Joe's pinched!" she warned him.[33]

At 12:30 p. m., Frank and Ora fled from Frank's home.[34] About this time, a torn police cap the same size as Dillon's and an auto floor mat with bloodstains were found.[35] That night, Roy led the police to Frank's home at 1907 Bremen Avenue, where they arrested Frank's wife. Later a coat was found and identified as having been worn by Roy during the double murders.[36]

The next day, a young girl saw a fresh mound of dirt surrounded by blood with a foot protruding from a culvert and went to her father, a farmer. He dug up the body and called the police.[37] The thirty-nine-year-old Dillon, a bachelor, had been a valued member of the police force since 1908. A total of $960 in reward money was offered by several individuals and organizations.[38] The St. Louis police later recovered more than $100,000 in stolen property and money from the Lewis home.[39]

The police chief also issued an order about garages and sheds:

> *You will have a thorough and systematic canvass immediately made of your district to ascertain by whom and for what purpose sheds and garages are being used.*
>
> *It has developed recently that sheds in various parts of the city have been used as fences for stolen property, especially stolen automobiles.*
>
> *Patrolmen should be informed as to the character of all such places on their beats and in future must see that prompt action is taken following the discovery of an illegitimate business.*[40]

THE ST. LOUIS UNDERWORLD

Thomas Egan was the most powerful gang boss in St. Louis in 1916. According to one writer, "Egan had all of the qualities of the ideal crime boss. He was quiet, powerful, patient, resourceful, connected, popular with the troops and public, imaginative, and often thoughtful about the future." Three years earlier, he had seized control of city politics and made no secret that he was the political and criminal leader of St. Louis. Egan bragged to a *St. Louis Post-Dispatch* reporter that more than four hundred men were in his gang. His saloon served as his headquarters. Sometimes the police would raid the saloon after the murder of a gangster, but this was just for show. With a lot of fanfare, Egan's thugs would be taken to jail, but they were always released quickly and quietly. They became known as "Egan's Rats" after an officer used that term to refer to them.

Before Prohibition, which Egan saw coming, St. Louis had strictly regulated the liquor business. Since the mob boss and other gang leaders wanted to have peace, they set territories for each gang and planned to supply liquor to St. Louis citizens from many large cities. Arrangements for the security of the liquor shipments were made.

Egan let the police crackdown on the small and weak city gangs (such as the Lewis- Jones Gang), which gave the impression that something was being done to control crime. In return, the police left the "Egan Rats" alone. In April 1918, before Prohibition went into effect, Tom Egan died; his brother William became the new gang leader.[41]

CHAPTER 6:

THE CONFESSION

On April 11, 1916, while going to Kirkwood, Missouri, for a St. Louis County inquest into the murders of McKenna and Dillon, Roy Lewis mentioned his brothers Frank and Ora. According to the gangster, they would not be caught without "some shooting," and Ora was a tough "dead shot" who could hit a dime at twenty yards.

Handcuffed, Roy was taken into a crowded St. Louis County inquest room at Kirkwood City Hall by two detectives at 10:40 a.m. The crowd refused to disperse. Scowling people in the crowd made the murderer nervous. Nevertheless, the inquest began twenty minutes later. William Wilson, the farmer who uncovered Dillon's body, and his ten-year-old daughter, Helen, testified about finding a foot protruding from a fresh mound of dirt.[1]

"They've got him out here, but they'll never take him back," a man in the crowded inquest room yelled. "He'll never get back to St. Louis alive," another man shouted.[2] According to the police, who were confident they could protect their prisoner, the violent talk was not in any way "staged."

Since Roy Lewis wanted to return to St. Louis to make a statement to Chief of Detectives Samuel Allender, the inquest was adjourned for at least two days, and the criminal was taken back to the city. Before noon Lewis reached Chief Allender's office. Roy hoped the police would release his mother and sisters if he cooperated. Officers told Lewis that anything he said would be "used against him." With Allender asking the questions, the gangster gave a detailed murder confession before several witnesses beginning at 11:50 a.m. Although the confession could not be used against him in court, it provided much information about many crimes.[3]

According to Roy's confession (which differs from the accounts of eyewitnesses):

> *We talked with Frank a minute and decided to throw both machines away. We also decided that I should stay there and clean up a bit and go out and see what was found out. I stayed in the house, washed up and had some breakfast and went back into the garage to get my overcoat.*
>
> *Frank and Ora had left, each taking an auto, and in about three-quarters of an hour they came back with a car and ran it into the garage.*
>
> *Ora looked out into the alley and seen [sic] a policeman coming down the alley. I wanted them to come on and ran away and leave it there. I said:*
>
> *"Come on, let's go out the front way and he will never see us." I went right on out and Ora was in the door and I thought they were coming. I went into the house and they never came up to the house.*
>
> *I was in the kitchen and looked through the curtains. I saw the policeman's hat as he came down the alley. After five minutes I thought the officer must of gone by. I returned to the garage after Dillon was murdered and saw the policeman wrapped up in a blanket. They discussed what they should do.*[4]

As Roy was giving his confession, Detective Sergeant Frank McKenna, an uncle to the murdered John McKenna, entered the room and looked hard at the prisoner. The officer was made to leave for fear he might interrupt the confession.

Roy attempted to put the blame for the murders on his absent brothers. Guarded by several detectives led by the chief of detectives, Roy confessed that his brothers Frank and Ora had killed McKenna and Dillon. He admitted he was present when the motorcycle policeman was slain and that Ora and Frank murdered Dillon. Roy said he had helped put the body and a bloody spade into a vehicle, but denied he helped murder Dillon. He also insisted he had not gone with his brothers when they removed and buried Dillon's body.

According to Roy, the Lewis boys had carjacked E. G. Beach's automobile in front of the St. Regis apartments in February and had forced Beach and his wife to drive them through Kansas City. He denied they had murdered Samuel Brown, a cab driver killed one night when responding to a call, or officer William Koger, killed three years before. The taking of the confession continued until four thirty in the afternoon, with a half-hour lunch break, and then Roy signed it.[5]

Later, Chief of Detectives Allender was asked how he made Roy confess. He said: "Just like a good reporter gets the story he is sent after, by constant digging. We used no third degree, no sweating and no electric chair methods. We did not hypnotize him. It was just a case of hard work, just digging until he finally weakened and wanted to tell his story and ease his mind."[6]

City lawyers decided that since Roy showed in his confession that he was present with his brothers at the time of the murders and had helped to remove the body, he was guilty of first-degree murder.[7]

Even after he had finished confessing, Roy continued to talk. "The St. Louis police are right on the job," the criminal remarked. "They were after me almost as soon as my wife and I got here with the jewelry that we got when we caved in a store window in Kansas. The Lord only knows how Ora and Frank and I got away that night in Beach's car….it seemed as if we saw a policeman every block. When Frank, like a fool, fired at a policeman, the policeman didn't turn, but fired right back."[8]

That day the police continued their investigation of the double murders. The coat found wrapped around Dillon's buried body was determined to be Ora's, connecting him to the officer's murder. Eyewitnesses to McKenna's slaying identified the coat as the one worn by his killer. A tailor named Henry Kribs, who owned the house where the Lewis family lived and had leased it to them some four months before, told police: "There can't be any mistake about that coat. I didn't make it, but I know it well. It is the coat that was worn all winter by Ora Lewis, or 'Mutt Lewis,' as he was usually called."[9] The tailor also indicated that the bloodstained hatchet found near Overland Park, Missouri, Sunday afternoon was from the Lewis home. According to Kribs, the numerous automobile accessories found in the Lewis home had not been there when the family had leased the house. The Lewis family counterclaimed that the items had been in the house when they leased it.[10]

PANCHO VILLA

In January 1916, a group of Americans were shot at by bandits in Chihuahua, Mexico, and on March 9 some of Mexican revolutionary Pancho Villa's men raided Columbus, New Mexico, killing some Americans. Villa was held responsible. President Woodrow Wilson ordered a punitive expedition under General John Pershing to capture Villa dead or alive. The expedition, from March 1916 to February 1917, was a failure.[41]

CHAPTER 7:
THE INQUEST

The St. Louis city inquest into the murders of McKenna and Dillon began in the coroner's room on April 12 at 9:15 a.m. Steps were taken to handle emergencies. Afraid that someone might attack Lewis, Coroner Padberg ordered every person in the room to be searched for weapons before the testimony began. They all had to stand up while officers examined their clothes. Anyone entering later was searched at the outer door. Sitting in a corner near the coroner's jury and surrounded by officers, Roy Lewis was excited and nervous, especially while the crowd was being searched for weapons. Men stood on the radiators in the crowded room.

Lewis crouched with his manacled hands in front of him. Shabbily dressed, the sleepy murderer was haggard, with a growing beard and feverish eyes. The criminal later settled down. Often he whispered comments to detectives and kept a close watch on each witness. Just after noon, Lewis was called to the witness stand. The coroner told him he did not have to make a statement.

"I want to make a sworn statement," Lewis replied.

As Lewis raised his manacled hands, he was sworn in. He took the stand for fifty minutes, giving the same account of the murders that he had given in his confession. Coroner Padberg and Assistant Circuit Attorney Baer tried to show that Roy Lewis's role in the murders was greater than he stated. The criminal was cool and with great skill defended himself. He enjoyed talking about the criminal exploits of the Lewis boys. The crowd surged forward to get close to him and loudly laughed at his occasional jokes. In response to questions from Coroner Padberg, Lewis went into detail about the movements of his brothers when McKenna was murdered. Roy denied they had told him the officer was dead. He had seen a bloodstained hatchet on the ground and a bloodstained shovel leaning against a car.

"And still at that time you didn't know Dillon was dead?" the coroner asked.

"I didn't know he was dead," replied Lewis.

When the coroner asked him if he had seen bloodstains on the kitchen door, the nervous Lewis did not answer right away. There could not have been any bloodstains, Roy believed, since his brothers had no signs of blood on them. Perhaps, he suggested, it was meat that had been dropped. He did not remember any bloodstained clothing or gun found in the house.

"Were you or were you not present when Dillon was slain?" asked the coroner.

"I was not," he answered.

The gangster insisted he did not made any effort to attract the attention of McKenna at the gas station so that Ora could shoot the officer.

Assistant Circuit Attorney Baer asked him if the gang could be taken alive. At first Roy said his brothers had plans to seize and grab the gun away from any policemen who tried to arrest them, and his motorcycle would be destroyed. They might tie the officer to a tree somewhere in the country, he said. The criminal insisted his brothers would submit to arrest if they could not get away, but later had to admit he told Chief Allender the opposite.

There were many false reports on the whereabouts of the Lewis boys. Roy insisted he did not know where his brothers were and that they had made no plans to get together. The police could not find them, but hoped the Lewis family would lead them to the criminals. Roy remarked to a detective that he might reveal where his brothers were if his mother, two sisters, and niece were set free. Roy said his brother Oscar, who had not been with them for some time, had recently worked on a farm near Carlinville, Illinois, but he had not recently heard from him.

Witnesses and Roy himself identified a revolver and a coat as belonging to Roy. But according to Roy, Ora killed McKenna, and Ora and Frank later killed the patrolman Dillon.

"They did many things just because it was a lot of fun," Roy remarked.

His family had lived like gypsies for years, he testified. But for the last two years, the Lewis boys had provided for the family without telling them the source of the money. Roy admitted he had lost some money gambling.[1]

"You didn't think your brothers would let him [Patrolman Dillon] get away from the garage, did you?" Roy was asked.

"I didn't know what they'd do," he replied.

His mother and sister Eva were taken to the witness room. Mrs. Lewis became hysterical and screamed, while Eva wept. Roy's stepfather did not attend the inquest. Frank's wife, Roy's sister Stella Landon, and Stella's daughter stayed at headquarters.

The first witness was twenty-two-year-old George Fisher Jr., the attendant at the gas station where Ora killed McKenna. The young man described what had happened and said that just as he got the police station on the phone, he saw the shorter man, Ora, shoot McKenna in the head. He had heard no request for a drink of water from Ora. Ordered to stand up, Roy was identified by Fisher as the tall man with the shorter Ora.

A chauffeur, Roy Smith, told of hearing the shot from outside the station. He said someone remarked, "There goes chiselchin," McKenna's nickname (given because he had a sharp chin). Smith pointed out Roy as the tall man, but could not identify from a photograph that Ora was the short man.

Clarence J. Conway told of hearing a shot as he was driving up to the station. He had heard Smith say, "There goes McKenna."

John Walker, a janitor, said he was in the alley at the gas station when he saw the arrest and heard the shot. "'Lord have mercy,' I said, "somebody's shot."' When asked if he had said anything to the two men as they ran past, the janitor said he "shorely [*sic*] didn't." Roy smiled and told a detective, "It was lucky for him that he didn't talk to anyone."

That night after the inquest, Lewis said to a detective, "They'll never get my brothers. They needed only two hours' start and they had two days. They are away out in the Cherokee Nation, in Oklahoma, by this time. They have hundreds of friends there who wouldn't let them be arrested."[2]

On the second day of the inquest, April 13, everyone going into the inquest room was once again searched for weapons. The crowd was smaller than the previous day. Several members of the Lewis family testified at the inquest, including Martha Bubb, Eva, Stella Landon, and Frank's wife, Jennie. Roy's wife had not been found.

Stella Landon, who lived at the Lewis residence, and Mrs. Bubb admitted that Oscar had been at the Lewis home on the day of the murders. This was the first time Oscar was mentioned as recently being in St. Louis. Roy had not implicated Oscar in the murders, and even claimed Oscar had not been in St. Louis for some time. Oscar had been working on a farm in Illinois, Stella testified, and had been away for some time, but she did not know where he was currently living.

Mrs. Landon was asked if bloodstains on the kitchen floor of the Lewis home might have been caused by meat from their meals. She said they had no meat for breakfast, sausage for lunch, and liver for dinner. Stella admitted that the coat found about Dillon's body had been on a hall rack in their home and everyone in the family had worn it. According to her, the revolver that killed patrolman McKenna had been in a kitchen drawer, but she did not know its ownership. There was also another small revolver in the house, she said.

Just before noon, Roy again took the stand. The bloodstained shovel, hatchet, and Ford car mat were shown to him. He believed they were similar to those he had seen in his home. Sterling E. Edmunds told of finding the bloodstained hatchet on the Sunday afternoon of the murders. A Captain O'Malley testified as to the disappearance of Dillon after McKenna was killed and the search of the Lewis home, where bloodstains were found.[3]

When Mrs. Bubb was questioned, it was learned she could neither read nor write. Warrants were requested for the Lewis family women that day—Mrs. Bubb, Eva, and Stella—charging them with receiving four stolen hams and a valise containing stolen clothing taken from a freight car in Alton, Illinois.[4] After testifying, Frank's wife, Jennie, told the detectives who were taking her to police headquarters, "I am done with Frank forever."

That night Roy told detectives the Lewis boys had been wearing clothing stolen from a rich young man named J. D. Wooster Lambert of St. Louis. His truck with his name on it had been stolen from a freight depot at Clayton, Missouri, about three months earlier. Smilingly Roy told the detectives, "This shirt I'm wearing came out of that trunk. It's Lambert's. He has kept us boys in clothing ever since. There were silk shirts and pajamas and a lot of other things I don't know the names of. The stuff we got out of that trunk would keep an ordinary man well-dressed for several years."[5]

On April 14, authorities continued to make precautions to guard Roy from possible attack, although the crowd again was smaller. Roy and John Bubb were sent to the coroner's office from police headquarters under heavy guard. A dozen officers protected Roy in the coroner's room, and everyone entering the room was once again searched at the door for weapons.

The fifty-year-old John Bubb testified during the morning that he had been married for about thirteen years to the mother of the Lewis children and had a very close relationship with his stepsons. Bubb had not seen Oscar the day of the murders and for a few days before. He had never seen the Lewis boys with guns, he said. Their stepfather admitted that a bloodstained blanket, in which Dillon's body was found, had come from their premises on Athlone Avenue.

Claude Soule, a farmer, was a witness at the inquest, and after viewing Roy closely, repeated his declaration that Roy was the one he saw riding a bicycle away from where the abandoned Hudson was at eleven thirty on the morning of the murders. The bicyclist passed him at very close range, and definitely it was Roy, he testified.[6]

When Roy took the stand again, he said he did not go into the country with his brothers after the killing of Dillon, denying that he was the one Soule saw. "If I'd been there," he insisted, "I would say so." Later, Ora admitted he had been the bicyclist.[7]

In response to other questions, Roy said the blanket found around Dillon's body was stolen, but he had forgotten from where. A brown coat at the house, Roy said, belonged to what he called "the company," which consisted of Frank, Ora, and himself, but not Oscar, who only did a few small "jobs" with them. However, Roy later confessed to Chief of Detectives Allender that Oscar was with them on the wire-stealing trip before the double murders. The "company," Roy claimed, agreed to "stick up" any policemen who came after them, but had no plans to kill them. He denied that Ora had remarked over Dillon's body, "We've killed the bull." Roy insisted Ora had only said, "We've got him."[8]

That day, after two and a half days of testimony, the city inquest jury found all the Lewis brothers guilty. The verdicts were as follows:

> *Patrolman John McKenna, 29-years-old, died at the city hospital at 9:50 a.m., April 7, of a gunshot wound of the brain, said wound being caused by a bullet fired from a gun in the hands of Ora Otis Lewis, alias "Mutt," in a filling station at 618 North Whittier street at about 7:50 a. m., April 7, 1916. We also find that Roy J. Lewis, alias Joe Lewis, was feloniously present and feloniously aiding, assisting and abetting in the commission of said act. Verdict homicide.*
>
> *Patrolman W. A. Dillon, 39-years-old, died in the garage in the rear of 4253 Athlone avenue from fracture of the skull (head crushed) due to being struck with a hatchet, shovel and other instruments unknown in the hands of Ora Otis Lewis and Roy J. Lewis, alias Joe Lewis at that time and place. And we further find that Oscar Lee Lewis is an accessory to the above crime. Verdict homicide.*[9]

As Roy was being taken from the Central District Police Station to the Municipal Courts Building on the afternoon of April 14, the father of the murdered officer Dillon, with his two other sons, tried to attack Roy, but he was subdued by officers. He was not arrested because he was unarmed.[10] Coroner Padberg immediately adjourned the hearing when he heard reports late in the afternoon that there might be attempts by friends of the murdered policemen to kill Roy. No one was allowed to leave the inquest room until the heavily guarded murderer was taken in a patrol wagon to the police station.

After the inquest, Roy was in a silly mood. As the police patrol wagon pulled up to police headquarters, he asked the chauffeur what kind of vehicle it was.

"A Locomobile."

"It looks like a pretty good one," Roy replied. "Loan it to me for five minutes."

The next morning, April 15, Roy remarked to one of his guards, "I wish you would get me some smallpox germs. I want to break out." He had recalled that his brother Ora had been arrested in 1913 in a small Missouri town and became ill with what looked like the smallpox. He had escaped from the pesthouse after being sent there from jail.[11]

In the office of Chief Allender, Mrs. William Anderson of St. Louis identified Roy Lewis as a burglar who had entered her home the afternoon of March 21. He had taken two diamond rings valued at $164 and $125, plus a half dollar. She was certain he was the man when she heard him speak and remembered his slight lisp.[12]

Guarded by eight officers, Roy was taken in a patrol wagon to Kirkwood for the county inquest that day. Other policemen followed in another vehicle. Eva and Gertrude Landon went under guard in a third car. About ten witnesses were examined in the morning, all of whom gave the same testimony as at the city inquest. The spade and hatchet with which patrolman Dillon was killed and the blanket in which his body was wrapped were sent to the county inquest. After deliberating only ten minutes, the jury returned the same verdict as the city inquest, that Dillon was killed by Roy Joe, Ora, and Frank Lewis, and that Oscar Lee Lewis was an accessory to the crime. Roy and the two women were returned to St. Louis.

Many curiosity seekers, mostly women, went to the St. Louis city central district jail to see Roy that afternoon. The throng was so large that some were barred. For about two hours, the visitors filed through the holdover and went past the criminal's cell, but were not allowed to talk to him. Often Roy, who greatly enjoyed being the center of attention, stood at his cell door with light from the outer windows displaying his full face. In the afternoon, reporters were allowed to talk to him, as long as they did not question him about his crimes. He talked about his life, but said nothing new.

That night Roy uttered his only expression of regret when he was moved from one cell to another to give women prisoners a chance to make their Sunday toilet. "Joe, we're moving you around a great deal, aren't we?" a detective said. "Yes," replied Roy. "I'm sorry this all happened."

On April 16, the grand jury took up the McKenna and Dillon murders. Transcripts of testimony given at the inquests were sent to the grand jury. Important witnesses testified in front of the grand jury.[13]

CHAPTER 8:

"WE BOTH DECIDED WE BETTER BLOW TOWN"

Meanwhile, surviving gang members Frank and Ora had fled from Frank's home at twelve thirty in the afternoon on the day after the murders of the two police officers.[1]

Ora later said:

> *In St. Louis, after the two cops were bumped off, I stayed over in Frank's house. The next day we read the papers. They were full of the murder . . ..*[2]
>
> *About 8:30 that morning Frank's wife, Jennie, telephoned to our home on Athlone Avenue to see if [Roy] Joe was there…but that a man got to the phone at the Athlone Avenue house and asked her what she wanted and she hung up the receiver…*
>
> *We had Frank's wife call up Union Station to find out what time we could get a train to Springfield, Missouri. We sent her down to Union Station after two tickets to Springfield, Missouri, but she got them for Springfield, Illinois…*[3]

> *We both decided we better blow town. We went to the Union depot and bought two tickets for Springfield, Mo. We waited around there about three hours for a train.*
>
> *The bulls and dicks were every place. They were watching the trains, so we could not get away. But we just walked through the gate, climbed on the train and rode to Springfield. We read the newspaper accounts of the killing on the way.*
>
> *There were a big bunch of dicks at Springfield watching the train. We just walked past them, ate a meal at the depot restaurant, and then went out to see the town. Springfield's a good town, but we wanted to look over the country a while before going home.*[4]

On the same train, they next went to Seneca, Missouri, and then to Oklahoma, where they visited the towns of Wyandotte and Sapulpa. Later they walked four miles to Kiefer. They then took trains to Henryetta and Ardmore, where Frank sold his watch and Ora sold a pair of cuff buttons, and finally to Shawnee."[5]

Ora continued:

> *The funniest thing happened at Shawnee, Ok. We bought a paper and were reading it. Our pictures were all over the front page. Some big guy with chin whiskers and a badge labeled "constable" on his coat, asked us what we were doing.*
>
> *"Just reading," we told him. He glanced over my shoulder, read the story about the crime and the reward, saying:*
>
> *"I'll bet if those tough birds come through here I'll nail 'em. There ain't none of them rough guys got by me."*
>
> *We thought it was funny, but we blew the town anyway.*[6]

They rode the rails from Shawnee to St. Louis, Missouri. While there they got a St. Louis paper and saw their pictures in the paper and read about Roy's confession. They then went to Oklahoma City. While reading part of Roy's confession, a well-dressed man came toward them, so they walked down the track and burned the paper.[7]

St. Louis police had followed the Lewis brothers to Ardmore, Oklahoma. Detective Frank McKenna, uncle of the murdered motorcycle officer John McKenna, learned a day or two later that the Lewis boys had purchased tickets for Springfield, Missouri, but the boys had departed. Then McKenna traveled to Oklahoma City, where the trail was completely lost.[8] When their money ran out, the bandits went from Oklahoma City into western Kansas on a freight train. They did not stop at any place for more than a day and finally went to Kansas City, Missouri.[9]

About three thirty on the morning of April 20, 1916, Frank and Ora were surprised while robbing suburban Wichita grocer Wilbert T. Tatman. His burglar alarm warned him that burglars were at work for the fourth time in three months and the seventh time in five years. The grocer, with a shotgun, and his son, sixteen-year-old Wilbert Tatman Jr., with a .38 revolver in each hand, rushed onto the porch of their home next door to the store. Ora was doing "picket" duty behind a cottonwood tree in front of the store and fired a shotgun at the grocer. "Frank! Frank!" he shouted.

Tatman ducked behind a large porch pillar, with his son behind him. The grocer's leg, sheltered only by a thin night robe, protruded and was struck by the rain of shot that splintered the pillar and flooring of the porch. All guns of the Tatman forces responded. As soon as Frank was safely away from the store, Ora ceased firing, and they fled. A dozen revolver shots were fired at them. Neighbors heard one of the men yell as if from sudden pain and saw him drop a ham taken from the store as the pair ran. Tatman believed one of his shots had taken effect.[10]

The outlaw brothers stole about six cars in the Kansas towns of Topeka, Wichita, and Lawrence, and in Denver, Colorado, and Cheyenne, Wyoming. The cars were each disposed of in other cities.[11]

Late in May at Marionville, Missouri, Frank and Ora visited Frank's mother-in-law, who told them, "You boys better get out of the country, there is a $5,000 reward for you dead or alive." The next day they went to Joplin to see their wives "to show 'em some time" and made a date with them for that night to go out riding for about three hours. They left for about ten days, then went back to Joplin, where they saw Jennie, Frank's wife, around June 1. The brothers gave her money for a trip to St. Louis and five dollars for "the folks." That was the last time they saw her.[12]

Ora ditched his wife when he suspected her of planning to turn him over to the police. As he later said, "But my wife tried to turn me up to the St. Louis 'dicks' when she heard there was an $1800 reward for my arrest. She showed 'em one of my letters from Joplin. After that I ditched her."[13]

Tired of the small-town life, they went back to Kansas City, Missouri, in June. From there the gangsters headed to Chanute, Kansas, where they stole twelve sacks of sugar out of a depot warehouse. They sold the sugar in Frontenac, Kansas, to a "Dago" (an Italian) named Sam, who ran a store there. Later the gangsters stole twenty-five cases of whiskey out of a warehouse at Minden, Missouri, and sold it to the same fence, Sam.

In a stolen Cadillac, Frank and Ora went back to Kansas City, Missouri. From that time, they were in and out of Kansas City. The "boys" would occasionally steal a load of whiskey at Minden and sell it in Frontenac. They would drive into the country and sleep in the car or on the grass. At no time did they rent a room.[14]

Ora later told the Kansas City police chief:

> *We soon got a couple good chickens, though, chief. They're some nifty kids. Used to be in vaudeville, a trapeze act, and they're the goods.... We kept up our motor car business. Only copped about six altogether, though. But, chief, people in Kansas City are mighty careless about their tires. We done a thriving business in tires. They're easier to handle and hard to trace.*[15]

In Kansas City, Missouri, in early July they took a four-hundred-pound safe out of a Standard Oil gas station after Frank broke the station door open. They put the safe on the running board of their car and carried it away. Ora put dynamite on the safe, then covered the dynamite with mud and rocks. When Ora set the dynamite off, it only blew the mud and rocks away, but did not blow the safe open. The outlaw drove back into the city, bought a hatchet from a hardware store, and returned. He knocked the bottom out of the safe in ten minutes. One hundred thirty-seven dollars was scattered inside the safe, along with a lot of papers.[16]

At Rosedale, Kansas, motorcycle policeman Fred Carr, out of uniform, was pursuing four men in a five-passenger Buick touring car, apparently for speeding, at one o'clock in the morning on July 10, 1916. Gardeners taking vegetables to the city market and several other people saw the officer murdered after three of the men stood up in the car and faced Carr. Suddenly a shotgun and two revolver shots were fired. Carr fell. A bullet had entered Carr's left chest just over his heart and another near his breast bone. His motorcycle wobbled and crashed into the curb. He fell unconscious and died a few minutes later. The car sped off rapidly and was swallowed up into the darkness. A doctor who lived nearby was called to the scene. The unmarried twenty-two-year-old Carr had been on the Rosedale police force for only two weeks. At first the identity of the killers was unknown. Later, however, the Lewis boys were considered suspects.[17]

Things were going so well in Kansas City that the "boys" and their girlfriends, Irene Bailey and Fay Southern, went on a one-day vacation to Cheyenne, Wyoming, during the city's Frontier Days celebration. They then traveled to Estes Park, Colorado, where the gangsters and girls fished and camped out for four days.[18] According to Ora:

> *Frank picked up a car and I gathered a lot of tires. I peddled the casings to the Junk dealers and kept the inner tubes. We left a trail of inner tubes all through Kansas, Colorado and Wyoming. Whenever we ran shy of dough we peddled an inner tube. They're better than travelers' checks. Everybody'll buy 'em, and no questions*

> *asked. We sold five one afternoon to a Kansas preacher. We took the girls with us, and we had a real vacation.*[19]

Returning to Kansas City, Missouri, about the middle of August, they put the girls in a room at 812 East Fourteenth Street. Ora then became sick with a high fever. For two weeks Ora, in a car's back seat, didn't know where Frank took him. Finally he was so sick, they took a room at the same place that the girls were.[20] Ora continued:

> *I ate so much and drunk so many kinds of water on the trip that I got sick. Frank had to work alone. While Fay—Fay's my girl—nursed me. It cost Frank about $300. Some brother, eh? Frank'll stick to you from A to Aizzard. Irene—she's Frank's girl—she usta come over and see me all the time and bring me flowers. Sounds funny, don't it, chief? Flowers, flowers, for a bum like me! But I like flowers, and the girls knew it."*[21]

Fay and a Mrs. Bush, the landlady, took care of Ora while he was sick with typhoid fever for seven weeks. A doctor visited twice a day and once at night for three weeks. To pay for his doctor bills, Frank stole tires from parked cars.[22]

There was a $1,900 reward for Frank and Ora from Kansas City, Missouri. The St. Lewis County, Missouri, police offered another $1,000, the city of St. Louis offered $500, and the state of Missouri had a $300 reward. The governor of Kansas set up a total reward of $450 with $150 each for Ora, Frank, and Oscar Lewis.[23] The sheriff's office in Wichita posted a $3,450 reward.[24]

CHAPTER 9:

THE CAPTURE OF ORA LEWIS

For more than two weeks, Kansas City, Missouri, detectives had been looking for two criminals who engaged in stealing auto tires and selling them to a plumbing shop in the city. Three detectives, including Harry Arthur, watched the store. On the night of September 21, 1916, while two detectives went to eat nearby, Arthur went inside. A few minutes later, Frank Lewis arrived in a stolen car and went into the shop to talk to the plumber for several minutes.

After Lewis left and leaped into his vehicle, the detective approached him, showed him his police "star," and stated he wanted to talk to him. When Arthur told him he was under arrest, Frank grabbed a revolver from a car-seat pocket and fired twice, but the bullets did not explode. Driving away, he struck Arthur with the fender, knocking him down. Frank fired again, the bullet passing through Arthur's hat. The detective returned the fire, but his revolver misfired, and Frank Lewis got away.[1]

Meanwhile, an informer told Arthur where Ora was located. The criminal, out of his sick bed only about three days and still emaciated and weak, was visited by detectives Arthur and John P. Clifford later that night at his rooming house. While Arthur was talking to the landlady, Ora left the house by the backdoor.

"Arrest him," Arthur cried to his companion.

The criminal was taken into his room. He made a quick move to his waistband, and Arthur threw him on the bed. They found a loaded revolver in the top drawer of the washstand and a shotgun under the carpet beneath the bed. With Ora were the two brothers' girlfriends. Ora said his name was "George Rogers" and that he was a rock crusher. Clifford looked at Ora's hands and replied, "No, you don't work as a rock crusher."[2]

Two officers at police headquarters recognized him. They had a photo taken of the fugitive and sent it to the St. Louis police department for identification. Policemen from St. Louis traveled to Kansas City to view the criminal.[3]

On the following night, Ora confessed to many of the crimes he and his brother Frank had committed since the murders of the two policemen in April.[4] The next morning, September 23, after a phone call from the St. Louis police confirmed that the picture was of him, Ora admitted he had helped kill two St. Louis policemen. Two owners of a St. Louis confectionery shop also identified the picture as Ora Lewis; while in St. Louis, the Lewis boys occasionally took young women to the store for candy and ice cream sodas. When the picture was shown to Ora's sister Stella in St. Louis, she fainted.[5]

That day Ora said, "Well, you got me. I'm your man. Yes, I was mixed up in the killing of both the St. Louis policemen, but I didn't have anything to do with that Kansas City affair."[6] He was referring to the murder of Kansas City patrolman W. F. Koger in 1913. Convict Dale Jones had recently told authorities at the Missouri state prison that the Lewis boys had killed Koger. The brothers were also suspected of the murder of motorcycle policeman Fred Carr, which Ora also denied.[7]

For three hours, Ora answered questions from the police chief and a dozen detectives. Speaking of the two girls, Ora said, "You want to take good care of 'em, chief, for they are mighty good girls. They didn't have any idea about what Frank and me were doing."[8] According to Ora, Frank would never be taken alive. "Frank's a two-gun man, and he'll die with his boots on," he said. "He carries a bottle of cyanide with him, and if the worse comes to the worst, he'll take it."[9]

The gangster loved to read detective stories in magazines and books, but he had a very low opinion of lawmen of any kind. "They've all a bunch of boobs," he told the Kansas City detectives.[10] The police chief asked Lewis if he had any regrets for his life of crime.

"Not a bit, chief," he answered. "I've been at it since I was a kid, and it's second nature. Things just naturally stick to my fingers. But I'll take my medicine. You ain't heard me squeal and I'm not going to. I've had my dance, and now I'm ready to pay the fiddler. But take care of the girls, chief, they're good kids.

"Send me a package of cigarettes, will ya, chief? It's mighty lonesome down there in that hotel with those bums and drunks. They're not my kind, and I don't want nothin' to do with them."[11]

At ten o'clock that night, three St. Louis detectives arrived to bring the gangster back to St. Louis the next day.[12]

CHAPTER 10:

"WE ARE GOING TO BE POPPED"

On November 10, 1916, the trial of Roy Joe Lewis and Ora Lewis for the first-degree murder of officer John F. McKenna began before Judge J. Hugo Grimm of the Circuit Court for Jackson County, Missouri, with the selection of the jury. (Roy and Ora were not tried for the murder of patrolman William A. Dillon.) Thomas B. Harvey was the circuit attorney, Edward J. McCullen was the assistant circuit attorney, and Martin Weiss was the attorney for the defense. There were about fifty witnesses.

The state showed by direct testimony that Ora fired the shot that killed McKenna and that Roy was implicated in the murder by his presence there and the fact he was jointly engaged in the commission of a felony with his brother. Ora had said in his confession that he had no intention of killing McKenna, but that the revolver discharged by accident while he was trying to "stick up" the patrolman. After being in custody for four days, Roy had made a confession admitting that he was with Ora in the gas station. Saying he had entered the house just as Dillon entered the garage, Roy insisted he had had no part in the slaying of the patrolman.[1]

On November 15, the Lewis brothers at times had an almost listless attitude toward the proceedings, but were quick to smile when the testimony took a humorous turn. When John Walker, the janitor and preacher, described how when he heard the shot, he had exclaimed, "Lord, have mercy on my soul, there someone shot," the two brothers gave a hearty laugh. The laugh brought a sharp rebuke from Judge Grimm. "This a serious proceeding," he admonished, warning that a repetition would result in the clearing of the courtroom. The two defendants lapsed into a somber, half-bored expression.[2]

On November 21, a dramatic bit of testimony was given by Charles Bergmann, a ten-year-old boy, who testified to what he had seen in the garage where Dillon was killed. According to a newspaper account:

> *The boy, who began his recital on a hesitating, low voice, leaned forward on his chair, and as the climax of his story was reached—his description of the events in the garage—raised his right arm to illustrate how one of the brothers had lifted a shiny instrument. Then he raised both arms to illustrate how Dillon had tried to protect himself and told in a clear firm voice, which penetrated to all parts of the big room, that he heard Dillon cry, "Oh, don't: don't do that."*[3]

It was important testimony, for it was the only evidence that showed without any doubt that Ora and Roy had murdered Dillon. The brothers had blamed Frank for the murder. Ora's face became white, while Roy was dazed. Both shifted uneasily in their chairs, and Ora often looked at the floor until the boy finished his story.

The circuit attorney asked the boy several questions.

"What, if anything, did you hear?"

"I hear the policeman say, "Oh don't: don't do that."

"What else happened?"

"Then they closed the door."

"How many men did you see in the garage, Charles?"

"I saw two men."

"The policemen and two other men?"

"Yes, sir."

McCullen then ordered the two defendants to stand up.

"Tell me if you saw either of these men in the alley or the machine?"

"Yes sir: I saw both of them."[4]

Three days later, the state completed its case after Circuit Judge Grimm ruled that the confessions and admissions made by the outlaw brothers were not admissible. The judge told counsel he was reasonably certain the statement Roy made at the coroner's inquests was not a voluntary one. He did not believe that Chief of Detectives Allender was involved in any of the alleged cruel treatment Roy testified he received after his arrest and before his confession. The gangster claimed he was starved into confession and that a scar he had on his lip was from a kick from a detective, both at the Newstead Avenue Station and at police headquarters. The state introduced Bertillon records of physical characteristics (a system of identification used in criminology) to show that Roy had this scar when he was arrested six months earlier on another charge.

Judge Grimm thought the police, in their zeal to solve a mystery in which two of their brother officers had been slain, may have been cruel to Roy. However, the truth as to what happened to Roy, the judge said, lay somewhere between the extreme testimony offered by both sides.[5]

On November 25, the defense surprisingly announced no testimony would be offered on behalf of the brothers after the state closed.[6]

The next day, the young Bergmann and his friend identified Ora as the man who closed the garage door and hit Dillon with a shiny instrument when the officer was killed. Ora denied this the same day.[7]

The following afternoon brought the opening of final arguments on both sides. A huge crowd stood three deep around three sides of the courtroom, and the area reserved for lawyers and court attachés was full. According to the defense, Ora's killing of McKenna was an accident. A large part of the state's arguments sought to convince jurors that Roy was equally guilty with his brother and that the act of one of the defendants was the act of both in that they had an understanding to aid one another to escape in case they were arrested.

On November 28, as McCullen demanded, in a dramatic close to his two-hour talk, the death penalty for both the brothers; Mrs. Bubb, Eva, and Stella wept. Although McKenna had taken away Roy's revolver and Ora had fired the shot that killed McKenna, McCullen said Roy was equally guilty of the murder.[8]

"It was no mere accident," McCullen told the jurors, "that Roy was in the stolen automobile which drove up to the oil-filling station. When that shot was fired he fled with the man who fired the shot, and where a conspiracy is shown, the law says that the act of one is the act of the other."[9]

The jurors were taken to their room to begin deliberations at 4:25 p.m.; they were out only four and a half hours. When Ora smilingly remarked on the way to the courtroom that he was sure to be "popped"—criminal jargon for hanging—Roy remarked that they would "go together."

About fifty people, among whom were fewer than half a dozen women, sat in the dimly lit and smoke-filled courtroom when the buzzer sounded sharply twice, announcing that the jurors were ready to report. No relatives of the Lewis boys were in the courtroom; two of McKenna's brothers were there. At 9:05 p.m., the death verdict was returned for the two Lewis boys. The largest surprise in the verdict, according to lawyers, was the death sentence for Roy. "Good," a spectator in the rear of the courtroom cried.

A few gasps were heard. With stoic indifference, the Lewis brothers received the verdict and made no sounds. The jaunty, defiant attitude Ora displayed throughout the eighteen days of the trial was almost gone, but turning halfway around to the spectator seats, he smiled weakly. Sitting rigidly in their chairs with not a muscle of their faces changed, the Lewis boys briskly jumped to their feet when deputy sheriffs came to take them to their cells.[10]

The next day, Martin Weiss filed a motion for a new trial that charged irregular practices, prejudice instilled in the mind of the jury by the display of bloodstained clothing, and various other allegations. The bloody blanket and shovel displayed to the jury were alleged in the motion to have stirred up the "mob spirit." Arguments for a new trial were held that week, but these and all other motions were rejected. However, the judge commuted Roy's sentence to life imprisonment.[11] The brothers entered the Missouri state prison during January 1917.[12]

THE MISSOURI STATE PENITENTIARY

The Missouri state prison, one of the oldest and largest prisons in the United States and the first one built west of the Mississippi River, was on the Missouri River bluffs just seven blocks east of the state capitol in Jefferson City. It was the only prison in the state. When the institution had opened on four acres in 1836, it could hold only forty inmates. Less than two years later, two men had to be put in cells originally built for one. By the 1920s, the prison covered forty-seven acres and was called "the bloodiest forty-seven acres in America." Tough discipline was practiced. Whipping, the ball and chain, cold baths, and the sweatbox were routine punishments.

In 1918 the State Prison Board, influenced by progressive ideas, took over the supervision of the institution. Among its numerous reforms were that prisoners were given low wages; inmates earned time off under the 5/12 rule (five months off for good behavior for every year of the sentence); the terrible punishment of being placed in the "rings"—being suspended by the wrists for a long time—was abandoned; the office of warden was removed from political appointment; and a few rehabilitative programs were added. Other improvements for prisoners were minor. Little attention was paid to education. Guards, who were political hirelings, had a high turnover rate, got low pay, and received little training.

Two woman prisoners, Kate Richards O'Hare and Emma Goldman, sent to prison for antiwar activities, had gone to "Jeff City" in 1919. They proved to be effective critics of the system, denouncing the unsanitary conditions and crying "slave labor." Their stories appeared in newspapers and magazines, and they wrote to state legislators and Congress.

The inmates still had twelve-hour workdays and such punishments as flogging. As before, all prisoners had to walk in lockstep to and from meals and work. There were still too few guards and rehabilitation programs. The food service and medical care were inferior. Drug trade, inmate violence, and open gang warfare were widespread.

The prison also remained a human warehouse, with the number of inmates increasing at an alarming rate. In 1913 there were about twenty-five hundred prisoners. Twelve years later there were five hundred more prisoners. About four thousand inmates were in the prison in 1929, approximately 80 percent over official capacity. Blacks, who suffered the worst overcrowding, were confined to one building—"A" Hall—where seven or eight men were crowded into cells meant for three. Women were located in a separate building.

From the 1880s to the 1930s, the prison was as much an industrial organization as it was a penitentiary. Labor for profit was the major part of the penal system. The superintendent of industries made more money than the warden. Although anything produced was sold to farmers at reduced prices, the state made big profits from it in part because little of the profit was spent feeding and clothing the inmates. Factories existed to make shoes, work clothing, and binding twine, as well as soap, gloves, and furniture. The vehicle-tag plant made state license tags and highway signs. In 1923, the warden's biennial report stated, "Healthy and proper rivalry obtains among the different factories so to which can best serve the state." By 1925 the prison was making about $5 million a year in profits.[13]

Photos are from the Pinkerton Detective Agency file at the Manuscript Division, Library of Congress

WANTED FOR DOUBLE MURDER

$1800—REWARD—$1800

For the arrest, delivery to officers of this department and conviction of **FRANK LEWIS and ORA LEWIS**, who, with a third brother, **ROY J. LEWIS**, under arrest, murdered Police Officers John F. McKenna and William A. Dillon of this department April 7th, 1916. Implicated with these three brothers, though to what extent is not known, is a fourth brother, **OSCAR LEE LEWIS.**

The above reward is for Frank and Ora Lewis. This department will pay $1,000 for their arrest and delivery; the City of St. Louis will pay $500 for their arrest, delivery and conviction, and the State of Missouri will pay $300 for their arrest, delivery and conviction. A proportionate amount of the reward will be paid for either Frank or Ora.

ORA LEWIS

Alias Otis Lewis, alias DeMorris, alias "Mutt"—21 or 22; 5 feet 8½ or 9 inches; 150 to 160; medium build; dark brown hair which may be dyed black; blue eyes; dark complexion; raised scar back of left hand and usually wears glove on this hand.

FRANK LEWIS

Alias DeMorris, alias Gray—24 or 25; 5 feet 8½ inches; 160 to 170; stocky build; dark brown or black hair; grey or blue eyes; medium complexion; vaccine scar upper left arm; tattoo of nude woman and crossed cannons on left forearm; small scar lower abdomen, left side; small scar in back below right shoulder blade; scar over left buttock; small scar 2nd finger right hand. Frank is said to have bullet scars in chest and right arm, leaving arm stiff so he can not raise it above shoulder. This description of bullet wounds, however, is not authentic. Finger print classification: 1 R io 6 / 17 T o

OSCAR LEE LEWIS

Alias Lee Lewis, alias DeMorris—29; 5 feet 7 inches; about 150; medium build; dark brown hair; medium complexion; color of eyes unknown, but right one is turned out; scar on right cheek.

Finger print classification: 13 U [illegible] / 17 R [illegible]

This photo taken March, 1914.

These four brothers comprised a band of desperate burglars, automobile and wire thieves that operated for some time in this section and in the West. Their crimes reached a climax in the wanton murder of the two policemen.

Two of the brothers were arrested by Motorcycle Officer McKenna on the morning of April 7th while they were in a stolen automobile filled with stolen copper wire. One of the prisoners shot and instantly killed the officer while he was telephoning for a patrol wagon. The robbers then escaped in the auto.

Closely followed by the other two brothers in another stolen machine, the four went to their home in another part of the city. In the garage there they attacked Officer Dillon, who had entered to investigate the presence of the two automobiles and killed him with a hatchet, afterward taking his body in a machine into the county and burying it in a ravine.

The pictures appearing in this circular are pronounced good likenesses of the men wanted. They were taken about one year ago.

When arrested wire me (stating whether requisition is demanded) and officers will be sent at once.

WILLIAM YOUNG, Chief of Police.

St. Louis, Missouri, April 17, 1916.

$3,450.00 REWARD

Wanted for Burglary and Murder. Officers are warned to take no chances with these men.

ORA LEWIS — FRANK LEWIS — OSCAR LEE LEWIS

Ora Lewis alias Otis Lewis alias DeMorris alias De Orman alias "Mutt", 21 or 22 years of age, 5 ft 7 or 8 inches 150 to 160 pounds, Medium Build, Dark brown hair which may be dyed black or bleached to a blond. Blue Eyes, Dark Complected. Has passed as a woman, and has a raised scar on the back of the left hand. May wear a glove to conceal this scar.

Oscar Lee Lewis, alias DeMorris, alias DeOrman, 29 years old, 5ft. 7 inches tall, about 150 pounds, Medium build, dark brown hair, medium complexion, color of eyes unknown but right one is turned out. Scar on the right cheek. Finger Print Classification-13-17; 1-R; [illegible]; 15-16.

Frank Lewis, alias DeMorris, alias Grey, alias De Orman, 24 or 25 years of age, 5ft. 9 or 10 inches tall, 160 to 170 pounds, medium stout build, Dark brown or black hair, Grey or Blue Eyes, Medium Complexion. Vacine scar upper left arm, tattoo of a nude woman and crossed cannons on the left fore arm. Small scar lower abdomen, left side, small scar in back below the right shoulder blade, scar over the left buttock, small scar second finger of the right hand. Frank is said to have bullet scars in chest and the right arm leaving the arm stiff so that he cannot raise the arm above the shoulder. This discription of bullet wounds is not authentic. Finger Print Classification. 1-17; R-T; 10-0; 6.

These Three men accompanied by their brother (who is now in jail) came to Wichita and on the night of May 24th, 1915, killed one Officer and wounded another and made their escape. Were traced to Long Beach California and returned to Wichita and on the night of October 9th, 1915, killed a Grocer and wounded one of his clerks and escaped in an auto. On April 7th, 1916 they killed two officers in St. Louis, Mo. and escaped to Ardmore, Oklahoma and on or about the 20th of April 1916, they were surprised while robbing a suburban grocery in Wichita and again wounded a grocer and escaped and were traced to Durand, Oklahoma, where they sold a stolen auto and started for Detroit, Michigan. They were recognized in Detroit by parties who had known them in St. Louis and escaped from Detroit on the night of August 12th, 1916. They have talked of going to Buenos Aiers, South America or British South Africa. Watch all ports of entry and please post all Steam Ship Companies to be on the lookout for these men. Sometimes they go as ordinary tramps (watch Hobo Camps) and jungle up. At other times they are swell dressed and pass as (Moll Buzzers) and may be found around sporting houses or saloons, especially where there is music. When last seen they were well dressed and had plenty of money. They are of French Canadian parentage but born in the United States, speak French and Spanish or Mexican.

WATCH all garages and recruiting stations. Notify all Banks to watch for $2.00 bills highest serial number M82929299.

(See The Detective) for Reward offered by St. Louis)

Sedgwick County Kansas offers $1200 and the State of Kansas $450, for these mens arrest and conviction. An effort is being made to increase the Total Reward to $5000. If arrested ascertain if they will return without requisition. Hold and wire me at my expense.

Detective F. W. STEVENS,
Sheriff's Office,
WICHITA, KANSAS.

[illegible] Edition,
Sept. [illegible], 1916.

Reward circular sent out for the capture of the Lewis brothers

WANTED!—$2,000 Reward!

HENRY J. CLAYTON.

ROY D. SHERRILL.

TRAIN ROBBERS

These men are wanted in connection with the hold-up and robbery of the Kansas City & Denison R.P.O. (M., K. & T. Ry) train No. 27, at Koch Siding, three miles south of Paola, Kan., July 10, 1918.

HENRY J. CLAYTON'S description: Age about 32; height about 6 feet; weight 250 pounds; dark brown hair, cut pompadour; hazel or gray eyes; round, full face, usually clean shaven, but when last seen was growing a stubby mustache; blurred tattoo mark or scar from wound on right forearm; wears size 17 shirt; has large abdomen and wears belt low; usually wears black button shoes with bulldog toe; smokes cigars constantly and passes as oil man.

ROY D. SHERRILL, alias CHARLES D. GILLINGS, alias CHARLES A. ROLLINGS, alias GABE PRICE; Age 21; height 5 feet 10 inches; weight about 150 pounds; light hair, but may be dyed black or brown; blue eyes; slender build; long neck; nose somewhat flat; light complexion; wears size 14 shirt.

Under the Postmaster General's "Notice of Reward," dated August 3, 1916, $1,000 is payable for information leading to the arrest and conviction of any person on the charge of robbing the mails while being conveyed in any mail car attached to a railway mail train in violation of Section 197 of the Penal Code. It is believed that there were seven men connected with the hold-up of the train, and the railway and express companies have always paid liberal rewards for information leading to the arrest and conviction of any of these persons, in addition to the reward offered by the Post Office Department.

Should either of these persons be located, their arrest should be caused immediately and the undersigned at once notified by telegraph, "Government rate, collect."

JOE P. JOHNSTON,
Post Office Inspector in Charge,
Kansas City, Missouri.

KANSAS CITY, MO., July 25, 1918.

(5000)

WANTED—$3,000.00 Reward!

FRANK LEWIS — DALE JONES — ROY D. SHERRILL

TRAIN ROBBERS.

These men are wanted in connection with the hold-up and robbery of the Kansas City & Denison R.P.O. (M., K. & T. Railway) train No. 27, at Koch Siding, three miles south of Paola, Kansas, July 10th, 1918.

DESCRIPTION:

FRANK LEWIS, alias Henry J. Clayton, alias James Clayton, alias Frank DeMorris, alias Frank Rogers; age 28 (looks older); height 5 feet 9 inches; weight 250 pounds; coarse, dark hair; hazel or gray eyes; round, full face, usually clean shaven, but when last seen was growing a stubby mustache; blurred tattoo mark on left forearm; gunshot wounds in breast and right arm, (right arm stiff); wears size 17 shirt; has large abdomen and wears belt low; usually wears black button shoes with bull-dog toe; smokes cigars constantly and poses as oil or stock man.

DALE JONES, alias Lloyd Dean, alias Denver Dean, alias Charles Forbes, alias Ford Engles; age 21; height 5 feet 10 inches; weight 135 pounds; light chestnut hair (shows rather dark in picture); blue eyes; light complexion; middle finger on right hand amputated below second joint; dresses well, good mixer and pleasant manners.

ROY D. SHERRILL, alias Charles D. Gillings, alias Charles A. Rollings, alias Gabe Price, alias George Ryan; age 21; height 5 feet 10 inches; weight 150 pounds; light hair; light complexion (blonde); blue eyes; slender build; long neck; flat nose; wears size 14 shirt; flashy dresser.

All three of these men are experts at handling automobiles and usually drive cars of the Hudson, Cadillac or Marmon make.

Under the Postmaster General's Notice of Reward dated August 3, 1916, $1,000.00 is payable for information leading to the arrest and conviction of any person on the charge of robbing the mails while being conveyed in any car attached to a railway mail train in violation of Section 197 of the Penal Code. It is believed that there were seven men connected with the hold-up of the train, and the Railway and Express Companies have always paid liberal rewards for information leading to the arrest and conviction of any train robbers, in addition to the reward offered by the Post Office Department.

Should any of these parties be located their arrest should be caused immediately and the undersigned notified at once by telegraph, "Government rate, collect."

JOE P. JOHNSTON,
Post Office Inspector in Charge,
Kansas City, Missouri.

KANSAS CITY, MO., August 22, 1918.

(5000)

WANTED—$2,000 REWARD!

DALE JONES MARGIE JONES

MURDER and TRAIN ROBBERY

DALE JONES is wanted in connection with the hold-up and robbery of Kansas City & Denison R.P.O. (Missouri, Kansas & Texas Railway) Train No. 27, at Koch Siding, near Paola, Kansas, July 10, 1918. All other members of the gang committing this train robbery are either dead or in custody.

At Colorado Springs, Colorado, September 13, 1918, Dale Jones shot and instantly killed Chief of Detectives John W. Rowan, and wounded other officers while resisting arrest on the train robbery charge. He had entered the city in a Marmon automobile, accompanied by his wife, Margie Jones, and Roscoe Lancaster, alias "Kansas City Blackie." All three participated in the battle with the officers, and Margie Jones drove the automobile while making their escape. Roscoe Lancaster was subsequently killed while resisting arrest at Kansas City, Missouri.

DESCRIPTION:—DALE JONES, alias Ford Engles, alias Charles Forbes, alias Denver Dean, alias Lloyd Dean, alias Howard Layton, alias Felix Kingman. Age 21; height 5 feet 10 inches; weight 135 pounds; light chestnut hair, worn very long in front; light complexion—now pale and rather thin; middle finger on right hand amputated below second joint; dresses well, good mixer and pleasant manners. Speaks English and Spanish.

He is an expert chauffeur and automobile mechanic, and usually drives stolen automobiles of either Buick, Cadillac, Hudson or Marmon make. It is believed that he frequently disguises himself in women's clothing, at many times wearing a woman's hat and coat when driving automobiles. He is always heavily armed and is a very desperate character.

MARGIE JONES, nee Margie Celano, alias Jewell Dillon, alias Jewell Celano, alias Margie Dean, alias Margie Layton. Italian, age 20; height 5 feet 1 5-8 inches; weight 100 pounds; slender; olive complexion; black hair; brown eyes; ears pierced; speaks Italian, English and Spanish fluently; wife of Dale Jones.

She frequently drives the cars in which they travel, and in the battle with officers at Colorado Springs, Colorado, fired several shots with a revolver. Some two months ago she claimed to be pregnant, and it is possible she may be found at some maternity hospital.

Under the Postmaster General's "Notice of Reward," dated August 3, 1916, $1,000 is payable for information leading to the arrest and conviction of any person on the charge of robbing the mails while being conveyed in any car attached to a railway train, in violation of Section 197 of the Penal Code; however, the charge of MURDER pending against Dale Jones is the more serious offense, and he, with his wife, will be delivered to the authorities of the State of Colorado. The Commissioners of Colorado Springs, Colorado, have authorized the payment of a REWARD of $2,000, of which $1,500 will be paid for information leading to the arrest and conviction of Dale Jones, and $500 for information leading to the arrest and conviction of Margie Jones, his wife, upon the charge of the murder of Detective John Rowan.

Dale Jones and his wife, Margie Jones, are particularly desperate characters, and officers are cautioned to govern themselves accordingly when undertaking their apprehension.

Should either of these parties be located, their arrest should be caused immediately and the undersigned notified at once by telegraph.

JOE P. JOHNSTON,
Post Office Inspector in Charge,
Kansas City, Missouri.

H. D. HARPER,
Chief of Police,
Colorado Springs, Colorado

KANSAS CITY, MO., Nov. 2, 1918.

(10r

$100 REWARD $100

ROY D. SHERRILL, No. 13320

Alias ROY SHERRILL

Escaped from United States Penitentiary Reservation Leavenworth, Kansas, June 22, 1921

DESCRIPTION; White; age 25 years; height 5 feet, 10½ inches in bare feet; Weight about 140 pounds; light brown hair; slate medium eyes; complexion, medium; medium slender build; American; occupation, auto-mechanic.

RECEIVED at the United States Penitentiary, Leavenworth, Kans., November 13, 1918, from Fort Scott, Kans., under sentence of ten years for Robbing U. S. Mails and Theft from Interstate Shipment.

Bertillon Measurements: 179.2; 178.|-; 95.0; 19.7; 15.5; 13.6
6.7; 25.8; 11.5; 8.9; 46.7.

Finger Print Classification: 2 U OO / 24 — I

Marks and Scars: Scar ½ inch obliquely outer at border of upper lip, ½ inch to left of M. line.

This man is supposed to have escaped in a Ford Sedan, State of Kansas License No. 10336, engine No. 3975104. He is likely to be in civilian clothes. This man is a dangerous character and may offer resistance to arrest.

$100 Reward will be paid for his delivery after identification has been made, to an authorized officer of this Penitentiary.

Arrest and wire:
W. I. BIDDLE, Warden
United States Penitentiary
Leavenworth, Kansas

6—22—21

a visit from the Jones-Lewis bandit pack would drop the tasks they were engaged in, and their minds, ever ready to be diverted from the routine of counting money, or recording

(*Above*) Thomas Knight, (*right*) Roscoe "Kansas City Blackie" Lancaster, and (*below*) George Eudaley—three members of Dale Jones' bandit gang, all being killers and quick on the trigger

money transactions, would leap to the cause of the noise that had startled them. The disturbance, slight as it might seem in a banking room, would cause a kind of sluggishness in the minds of the people at work behind the cages, because of the suddenness of the change from one condition of the mind to another. Of course, it takes only the slightest fraction of a second for an active mind to pass from one situation to another, but the time required for the process was ample for the purpose of Dale Jones.

For the new impression—that caused by the coins ringing on the floor—was never fully registered on the mind of any employe of a bank about to be held up and robbed by Dale.

There was always a second situation—one which few people are capable of grasping! And that is, to look

one of the doormen, and ordered in a quiet voice to step aside, and stand with face to the wall, but without raising their hands. It always worked.

"Just stand over there, please, and act as natural as possible," the bandits would order, in tones that sounded like a request, but were, nevertheless, orders. A man's voice was a valuable asset in the opinion of Jones and Lewis. Eudaley and Sherrill usually acted as doormen, but when Kansas City Blackie joined the gang, he was posted at the door with Sherrill, and Eudaley worked the tills. This arrangement was made because of Blackie's shooting ability. One man was stationed at each end of the bank room, sweeping the length and breadth of the building with his gun. The two remaining members of the band would loot the vault and money tills. Dale himself worked the vault.

The entire job was performed in less than one-tenth of the time required to tell it. Many a person caught in a bank that was being robbed by the Jones gang, has marveled at the smoothness and rapidity with which the bandits worked. Few people were ever foolish enough to make a false move in the presence of the most notorious robber organization America has ever known.

The bandits had "cleaned up" Kansas City. The Sugar Creek Bank, the Industria

(Above) Thomas Knight, (Right) Roscoe "Kansas City Blackie" Lancaster, and (Below) George Eudaley--three members of the Lewis-Jones bandit gang.., all being killers and trigger-happy.

John Shead, murderer of Officer Samuel Queen, of Hume, Missouri. Shead was the man who gave Dale Jones his first "eye witness" lesson in cold-blooded butchery—a lesson which the young bandit afterward told Chief Walston was "a kind of terrible gloating something," as he watched Queen die

John Shead, murderer of Officer Samuel Queen, of Hume, Missouri.

explain to the police and newspaper men three years later when he was arrested and convicted on a burglary charge, welled up in the heart of Dale Jones as he watched Officer Queen sink down into the velvet cushion of the passenger coach seat; watched the head of the officer sag sidewise onto his broad chest that fast was becoming saturated with his life-blood. It was not horror, this something that he felt at seeing another mortal shot to death in cold blood, nor compassion toward the murdered man for the death blow that Fate, in the form of a murderous thief, had dealt him. It was a "kind of terrible gloating something," he told me just before being taken to prison—"unexplainable."

Jones and Shead had just stolen an

(Above) Ora Lewis, and *(right)* Roy Lewis, his brother, both convicted and sentenced to life imprisonment for the murder of two St. Louis policemen. Their career of crime was a trail of ruthless butchery

shot and killed Patrolman Koger. And it was just prior to this murder near Raytown, that another brutal slaying occurred, the witnessing of which caused young Jones to begin writing the history of his career in red.

ON returning to Kansas City, Dale renewed his acquaintance with John Shead, with whom he had worked as a box-

(Above), Ora Lewis, and (Right) Roy Lewis, his brother. Their crime career was a trail of ruthless butchery.

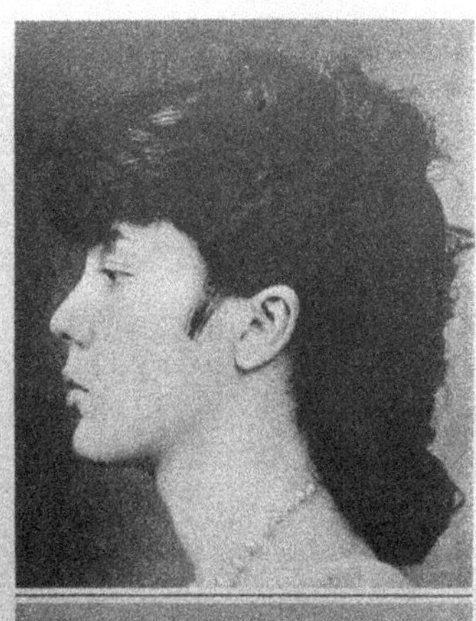

Dale Jones, Kansas City's desperate outlaw and (*right*) pretty Eva Lewis, one of his sweethearts, sister of the famous Lewis brothers. She frequently drove the car for the bandits during their hold-ups

Dale Jones, Kansas City's cross-dressing outlaw and (Right) pretty Eva Lewis, sister of the famous Lewis brothers.

"Can you picture what it would be to have your brother mount the gallows, with the executioner beside him; to have the black cap pulled over his eyes, to have the noose adjusted about his neck; to be asked if he had any last word to give to the world; to hear the intoning of a prayer for his soul—then to have the trap sprung, and your brother shot downward, earthward, till the cruel hemp draws tight with a snap, and breaks his neck?

"Can you picture your brother hanging there, limp and lifeless, his laughing eyes glazed and his gay voice forever stilled?"

"My brother will hang," the girl cries, screams, almost startling diners out of their chairs. A death-like hush falls over the vast hall that a moment before was filled with the noise of the merrymakers.

"Unless—*unless*—you will help me to save his life!" the pretty

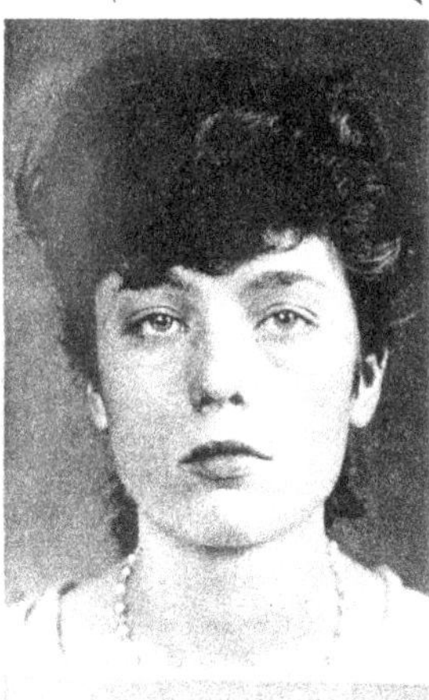

Two views of the notorious Eva Lewis, the drawing above being made by "Scottie" of the Wichita *Evening Eagle*, when she was at the heyday of her career as a cabaret singer and accomplice of bandits

Whether or not
Governor Gardne
influence on the C
was never
death senten
imprisonment
penalty in M
1918, and af
Missouri had
hang, in spite
punishment.
So we leave
Missouri State
by high, gray
they are to sp
Neither of th
parole, becau
pair to be ca
H. Livingston
Bureau of Cri
Jefferson City
governor wo
give the Lewi

We ret
bandit gan
bers of th
have now
pressions
something
unacquaint
type of m
But it was
Dale Jones' pack ever ex
fear. Even Blackie Lar
coward all his life, was
sociation with young Da
them, Eudaley, Sherrill, T
Lewis, was suffering from
Dale too, was getting imp
work to do, dangerous w
involved death itself.
Dale Jones furnished i
The Industrial State
robbed; the Sugar Creek
South Side State Bank was looted
The first robbery of the South S
Mattie Howard and her gang, an
lover, was killed.
The Jones-Lewis bandit gang sw
after robbery was committed, and
any of them. It was such a simple
Just saunter into the bank that h
place to be honored by a visit fro
time. The first man would walk
window, tender a large bill, and
break the note into small chang

Two views of the notorious Eva Lewis, a cabaret singer and accomplice of bandits.

to Wichita, while enroute to Kansas City. The murderers had been dogged by the law from one ... n Kansas City two days later. re said to have walked the entance. ving Frank to be in Kansas City, d Roy began making the rounds of es and speak-easys in search of their rother. They searched for several ut in vain, for Frank Lewis, ignorant ct that his brothers had returned to Kansas nd were desperately in need of assistance, reas far away from Kansas City as possible. He care for another encounter, such as the one he had had

in. Ora had been given a room on the ... voices in the hall, peered out to get a glimpse of ...

(*Right*) Mattie Howard, called "Queen of the Underworld," and (*above*) Marjie Dean, both sweethearts of the daring bandit leader, Dale Jones. Both these women were adepts with six-shooters, the latter being finally killed in a gun battle with the police

turned to his partner, and shoute "Stop that man! He is a broth man who shot my hat off!" Shoving the landlady aside, ficers sprang forward, and running after the fleeing m was overtaken just as he rea door, and in less than tw hours, the Kansas City pol releasing the prisoner to the authorities, to whom Ora m confession, not omitting the details of the slaughter o Dillon.

The cases of Ora and Roy L tried together in Circuit Judge court at St. Louis on Novem 1916. Roy was given life impr and Ora Lewis was sentenced to ha case was appealed to the Supreme Cou February 16th, 1918, the sentence of death firmed by that Tribunal. Date of execution w April 5th, 1918.

In the meantime, following the death penalty in

(Right), Mattie Howard, called "Queen of the Underworld," and (above) Marjie Dean, both sweethearts of the daring gangster leader, Dale Jones.

ie Hume constable's heart. Shead
er escaping from Queen at Hume,
o Rich Hill, which was carrying

's captor, Jones
n a window of the
went directly to
ks following the
ventured from
at agony of mind
weighed heavily
er-willed Shead,
cautiously from
out in the open,
rolled uptown to
He had barely
lighted corner,
ie clutches of
never forgets a

Attorney to refuse to issue a murd
Not an officer on the Force but kn
Jones was guilty, but then—what c
one man had seen the boy, and he
good description. And anyway, wh
the railroad man
derer? Wasn't it
a hobo, who was
pose of stealing
freight train? N
tectives with wh
search for box-ca
the shooting of th
So Dale Jones w
authorities, to sta
of Officer Queen;
the boy's acquitta
to go his way.
We again hear
weeks later, when
Roscoe ("Kansas
whose acquaintanc
easy operated by

Captain Frank Griswold, of the Wichita (Kansas) Police Department, who was shot to death by Ora and Roy Lewis during an attempted robbery of the A. E. Bump shoe store, in Wichita

Captain Frank Griswold of the Wichita, Kansas, police department, who was shot to .death by the brothers Ora, Frank and Roy Lewis.

like so many rats, creeping out only when the need for food necessitated it.

After weeks of confinement in the house, that had, so far, escaped the notice of the man-hunters, Dale Jones' love for excitement again manifested itself. He needed action, and adventure. So he proceeded to look for it.

Disguised as a woman, he went out each evening, called the police and gave them tips on where Dale Jones might be found. He would then stand on a street corner and watch the car of the short-call officers, as it sped through the crowded city to the fake address, where a mysterious informer had said Dale Jones was hiding. Each time one of these telephone messages was received, a squadron of officers was dispatched immediately to the address given as the hiding-place of the notorious bandit.

THE Kansas City police were being run ragged. There was nothing to do but to send out a carload of policemen every time one of these calls came in, as there was no telling when one of them might prove to be the real thing. There was too much money on the bandit's head to miss a chance of capturing him.

(Photo by Anderson Studio, Denver)

"Hello, that you, Ike?" came the laughing voice of Da Jones. There was no mistaking that voice, once you h heard it. "You can find me at 1500 Wyandotte Street in minutes. But don't send your men any sooner than that

Somehow, I knew that Dale Jones was not lying, when I added he had been in hiding on Wyandotte Street for the pa

(*Above*) Harry Lancaster, brother of "Kansas City Blackie" Lancaster. Harry committed suicide by hanging in the Nineteenth Street Police Station, Kansas City. (*Left*) Motorcycle Patrolman Luther McMahill, shot down in cold blood by the bandit chief, Dale Jones, on that eventful day, September 13th, 1918, when McMahill attempted to arrest Jones for breaking into a filling-station near Denver

several weeks, and I felt confident that the youthfu robber chief would be in our jail the next morning.

But again the swiftness with which Dale Jones moved had been underestimated, and this time, I was to blame when the raiding party returned to Headquarters empty-handed, but showing every sign of having been interestingly engaged out on Wyandotte Street. I sent out eight men, when I should have sent 50. The officers found the house all right, and they also found something else

EIGHT police officers stood about the same chance o beating the Jones-Lewis bandits in an open gun battl as so many high school boys, even when the bandits refused to shoot to kill.

Dale had rushed back to the house, after calling m and giving the tip on his gang, and warned the men tha the cops were wise. The two cars, in which the bandit had traveled over half the United States, in their fligh from the Federal officers, were in readiness long befor the party of officers arrived, and had been driven aroun the block. They now stood waiting, with Eva Lewis a the wheel of one, and Marjie ready to drive the othe machine out of Kansas City, as she once had driven th same big Marmon out of Los Angeles.

The house occupied by the bandits sat in the middle c a block, with vacant lots on either side. Tall bushes an weeds had grown up around the house, and in these the si

(Above) Harry Lancaster, brother of Roscoe "Kansas City Blackie" Lancaster. (Left) Denver motorcycle patrolman Luther McMahill, shot down in cold blood by the gangster Dale Jones.

ı impression of a raid participated in ıs than were actually present. Once oaches, no member of the gang was to long ›ut as ıt was e con- work- ıg the

ıs in- often to the ›ther by num- irteen, which ns to believe ›ered, at least,

·obbery com- gang, during t the band of through the ıp of the Mis- cas passenger without a hitch. thin a radius of of the lonely spot where the *Texas* :reamed" the next ery, in spite of the 'ar was at its peak, devoting column e to describe the front.

·ctly the bandits' system of calling to · worked out, one large daily, the next louble streamer" across the front page

unded when 13 Bandits ›ot Katy Flyer

rteen persons had actually participated ıdvanced the night of the hold-up by on, of Ossawatomie, after he had con- · investigation into the robbery, and he passengers on board. Nor was this other investigators, including those ·y the United States Postoffice Depart- ths to come, so thoroughly had Dale's ıstructions.

·ed dollars were secured from the mail but the loot taken from the passengers ling thousands of dollars in money and

:he night of the hold-up, the brushwood de Cygne River was combed by more

gospel. They believed him when Jones assured them he was leading his gang into a "new racket" from which they would reap greater harvests, with less danger involved.

But now the job had been pulled, and the Postoffice authorities, with that determination which characterizes that group of men, and sets the service in a class by itself, when it starts out to track criminals, took up the trail of Dale Jones and his pack of marauders.

To California, down through New Mexico, across Texas, into the Arizona desert, back through Nebraska, Iowa and Kansas, over the very route taken by the gang on that fateful night of the train robbery, two men trailed Dale Jones and his seven confederates. The bandits had no time to engage in robbery or plunder. All their days and nights were occupied with one problem—a problem that remained with

(*Left*) Dale Jones (*Below*) Chief of Detectives John Rowan ("Two-Gun Johnnie") of Colorado Springs, as he appeared shortly before his last gun fight. Chief Rowan was shot to death by Dale Jones, before the dreaded Colorado Springs officer could reach for his guns

18127

(Photo by Carl F. Mathews, Supt. of the Bureau of Identification, Colorado Springs Police Dept.)

(Left) Dale Jones, (Below) Colorado Springs, Colorado, Chief of Detectives John Rowan, who was shot to death by "Kansas City Blackie".

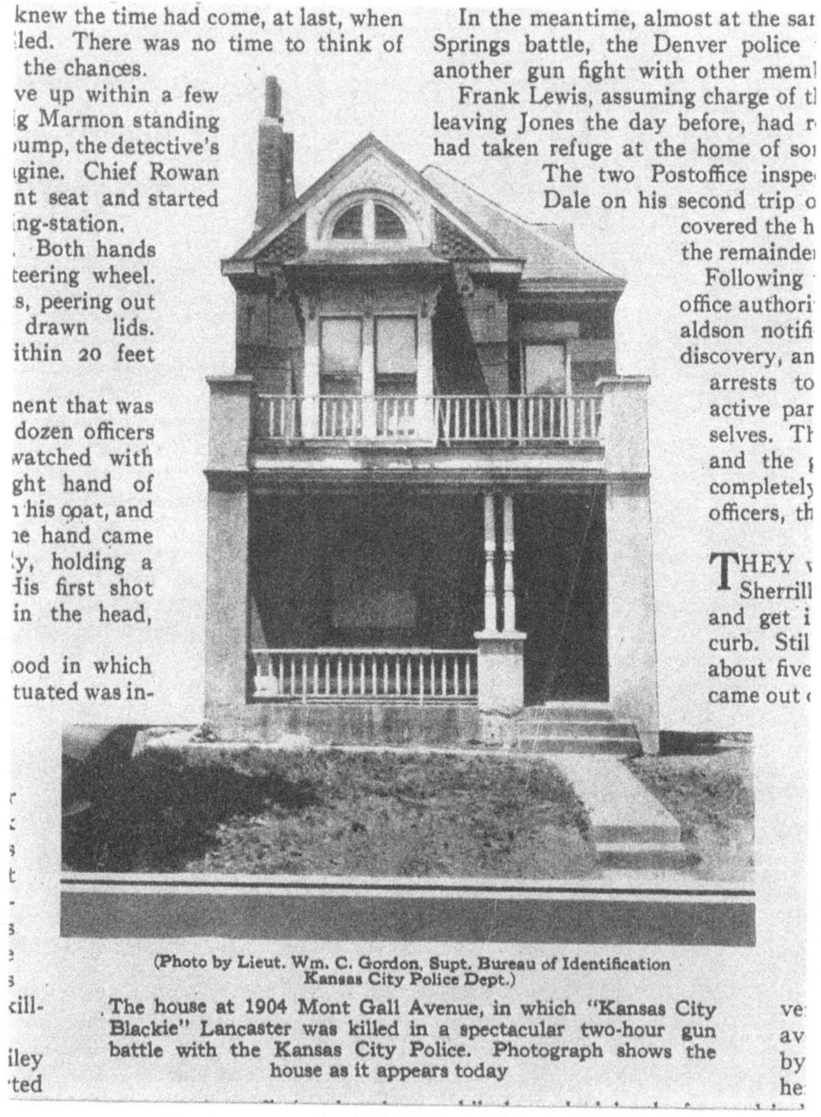

knew the time had come, at last, when
:led. There was no time to think of
the chances.
ve up within a few
g Marmon standing
ump, the detective's
gine. Chief Rowan
nt seat and started
ng-station.
. Both hands
teering wheel.
s, peering out
drawn lids.
ithin 20 feet

nent that was
dozen officers
watched with
ght hand of
his coat, and
ne hand came
y, holding a
His first shot
in the head,

ood in which
tuated was in-

cill-

iley
ted

In the meantime, almost at the sa
Springs battle, the Denver police
another gun fight with other mem
Frank Lewis, assuming charge of t
leaving Jones the day before, had r
had taken refuge at the home of so
The two Postoffice inspe
Dale on his second trip o
covered the h
the remainde
Following
office authori
aldson notifi
discovery, an
arrests to
active par
selves. Th
and the
completel
officers, th

THEY
Sherrill
and get i
curb. Stil
about five
came out

ve
av
by
he

(Photo by Lieut. Wm. C. Gordon, Supt. Bureau of Identification Kansas City Police Dept.)

The house at 1904 Mont Gall Avenue, in which "Kansas City Blackie" Lancaster was killed in a spectacular two-hour gun battle with the Kansas City Police. Photograph shows the house as it appears today

The Kansas City, Missouri, house, in which "Kansas City Blackie" Lancaster was killed in a spectacular two-hour gun battle with the Kansas City police.

The filling-station at Arcadia, California, where Dale Jones and Marjie Dean were shot to death by deputy sheriffs

The gas station at Arcadia, California, where Dale Jones and Marjie Dean were shot to death by deputy sheriffs.

PART TWO

CHAPTER 11:

THE LEWIS-JONES GANG

Frank Lewis had been busy recruiting a new gang from late 1916 into 1917. Lewis was the gang chief, with Dale Jones second in command; Roscoe "Kansas City Blackie" Lancaster, Roy Sherrill, John Shead, and Thomas King were members. Their goal was to steal a million dollars and liberate Roy Joe, Shead, and Ora.[1]

Convicts Shead and Jones had met Ora and Roy when the Lewis brothers entered the Missouri prison in January 1917. Since Jones had only six months left to serve of his sentence, he was asked by Eva during her frequent visits to the prison to contact Frank after his release in August 1917 and help free Shead, Roy, and Ora.[2]

Roscoe Lancaster, well known to police as a car thief, was born in April 1887 in Indiana to Samuel and Mary A. Lancaster. His brothers—Warren, Harry, and Louis—were also criminals. By 1900 his family was living in Kansas City, Missouri, where his father worked as a locksmith.[3] The 130-pound Lancaster, a butcher, was five feet five and a half inches tall, with black hair, hazel eyes, and a sallow complexion. In September 1912, he was convicted of second-degree burglary committed in Jackson

County, Missouri, and sentenced to four years in the Missouri State Penitentiary. He was received at the prison on November 20, 1912, and discharged on November 18, 1915.[4]

Roy Sherrill, a cabaret master of ceremonies and an auto mechanic, was born on September 19, 1896, in Sylvania, Indiana, to highly respected Baptist minister James L. and Louise Sherrill. Roy, who had come from a fine home, had a quiet disposition and was not considered "wild" or "dissipated."[5] With a brother, Sherrill had gone to work in the Kansas harvest fields in the spring of 1917. They visited Wichita, where they met Frank Lewis during drinking escapades.

One night that spring they became drunk, and Lewis and Sherrill decided to get "easy money." Their first job was to steal a bootlegger's car loaded with whiskey. They sold the liquor for $150 and divided the loot equally. The two criminals then robbed several bootleggers as they traveled in cars across the Kansas counties of Cherokee and Crawford with loads of liquor—a "very easy" job, for the victims did not dare to report the crimes to the police. Nevertheless, the puzzled authorities learned of them.

"We just held 'em and tied them hand and foot and then took their car and whiskey and sold it," Sherrill later said, smiling. "After a while we decided to take their cars whether they had whiskey in 'em or not. We rode in all kinds of cars and sold them with the skill of regular dealers. I had not learned yet of Lewis's ambition to get in 'big time stuff,' until we came to Kansas City. I learned it then and I also learned what a vicious criminal he was. He had it on me, and I knew it and did not squeal. Lewis also had a belief that a man was not a seasoned crook until he had committed murder. He tried to bring me to this, but I could not do it. He said he had killed thirteen men, and I believed him."[6]

Thomas King, who used the aliases Thomas Knight and Earl King, had been sentenced to two years for attempted burglary in Missouri in 1915. He had been received at the Missouri state prison on December 17, 1915, and was released on May 10, 1917.[7]

John Shead, born in 1888 in Kansas, was a laborer who had served time at the Hutchison Reformatory in Kansas and, before he joined the Lewis-Jones gang, was serving a life sentence for murder at the Missouri state prison.[8]

CHAPTER 12:

THE CROSS-DRESSING BANDIT

Born in May 1897 in Wichita, Kansas, to Paul and Elsey Jones, Dale Jones grew up in the Missouri woods and became an auto mechanic and a painter. His father was a carpenter, box-factory worker, and day laborer.[1] At five feet ten and an eighth inches tall, with blue eyes, a sallow complexion, and weighing 135 pounds,[2] the young criminal was a "good looking blond boy, with a disarming manner about him, and people did not take him seriously."[3]

A Los Angeles criminologist, Dr. Victor D. La Tour, talked to Jones in jail and reported that all of Jones's criminal acts were due to suggestion from others. The doctor said Jones was the most susceptible person to the influence of others that he had ever met. In one instance, the doctor wrote on a piece of paper, "You must write seven." He told Jones to write down any number between one and twenty without looking at the paper. Jones wrote down the number seven.[4] According to one account, "He was apparently a refined youth of quiet manners and neat appearance, and one who at once raised the question if some mistake had not been made in arresting him."[5]

Charles R. Burger, a Los Angeles city official, believed Jones had been wrongfully accused by the Missouri authorities of several crimes, ranging from murder to petty larceny. Burger wrote that Jones was "a quiet, soft-spoken, modest and courteous young man of 17, away above the average in intelligence, admired and liked by all who came in contact with him." But the young man himself boasted that "he had an uncontrollable desire to steal motor cars."[6]

As a young boy, Jones had often come before the Kansas City, Missouri, courts for various violations. At age thirteen, he fell in with the much older John Shead to steal from boxcars and railroad warehouses in Missouri. Police believed the two men killed Kansas City, Missouri, detective William Koger at a stakeout in the Kansas City railroad yards in 1913, but they could never prove it.[7]

The stakeout was set up because night after night, bandits had been robbing Missouri Pacific Railroad freight trains when they stopped at the Frisco crossing in Kansas City, Missouri. At nine-thirty the night of November 22, 1913, a fast freight train running from Pueblo, Colorado, to Kansas City was about due. Five men in a stolen car stopped on the track, turned off the lights, and leaped out. West of the track, three special officers for the Missouri Pacific—William Koger, a patrolman with a revolver; M. Barker, also with a revolver; and W. H. Boullt, with a pump gun—were hiding in a small railroad shanty watching.

Soon the freight was heard coming up the tracks. The three officers rushed out and ordered the bandits to surrender. Instead they fired at the officers with revolvers. Koger was able to fire one shot, but then fell when a bullet passed through his neck and into the back of his skull. As the bandits fled over the brow of a hill and fired at the officers, Boullt and Barker emptied their weapons. One of the robbers threw up his hands as if shot. Koger, a twenty-five-year veteran of the police department, died the next day. Only three months earlier he had resigned to be the house detective at the Hotel Baltimore, but soon returned to the police department.[8]

Two days later, Jones, who was wanted for stealing cars, was arrested at about four in the morning by Constable Samuel Queen at a Hume, Missouri, restaurant. The gangster was with Shead, who escaped. Jones's real name could not be learned, but the constable felt fully certain that he had a well-identified villain. Guarding Jones securely on that afternoon, the constable took him to Rich Hill, Missouri, and lodged him in the jail, with the plan of taking Jones to the Butler, Missouri, jail on the night train.

At ten thirty that night, Shead boarded the smoking car of the local Missouri Pacific train at Rich Hill. While the northbound train was being made up, the constable had his man securely shackled. As they sat in the smoker, Shead suddenly burst in on them from the rear, leveled a revolver on the officer and ordered him to throw up his hands. Instead Queen went for his revolver. Shead fired two shots. One entered the officer's left forearm, between the wrist and elbow. The second sent a bullet into the muscular part of his left arm, which ranged upward, lodging in the shoulder blade.

Railroad men and deputy sheriff Charles Horton rushed in and gave pursuit to the bandits as they ran through the forward door, with Jones handcuffed. Horton fired two shots, but without effect. Still chasing them, minus his hat and in a crouching position, Horton was discovered by night policeman Dan Lowery. Under the impression that he was one of the criminals, Lowery took two shots at Horton. Fortunately Lowery's shots missed and thus spared the deputy. When a bystander called out to Lowery that he was shooting at the wrong man, he stopped firing.[9]

Constable Queen was immediately taken to a local hospital and died about two days later.[10] According to a local newspaper:

> *It is a sad thing to contemplate that a good citizen—a man in the prime of life, and an officer in the simple discharge of his duty should be thus cut off from life, home, family and friends by a dastardly assassin.*

> *All law-abiding persons will extend their deepest sympathy to the bereaved family in this their hour of deep distress and hope for the bringing to speedy judgment of the black hearted slayer of Samuel Queen.*[11]

The two criminals fled to Kansas City, Missouri, and hid at the underworld hangout operated by Mattie Howard, "the girl with the Agate Eyes." Howard knew many of the Kansas City gangsters, including the Lewis-Jones gang.[12] For several weeks Jones and Shead stayed inside, but finally they left their hideout. Shead was the first to go out. He went uptown, where police caught him while he was window shopping.

On April 17, 1914, Jones disguised himself in a dress Mattie Howard had given him, masqueraded as a girl named Flo Engles, and went to Marshal's Drug Store in Kansas City, Missouri. At six that night, three detectives arrested "Flo"—too big for a woman—on suspicion of being in disguise. When they arrived at headquarters and were parking, the "young woman" tried to escape. The detectives grabbed the "girl's" dress as they tried to subdue her and discovered he was a boy. During their search of him, they found a large-caliber revolver in each hip pocket of the pants he wore under the dress. This was the first time Jones came to the attention of the public.

A local headline ran: "Youth who Passed for Woman Held in Murder Case."[13] Jones attempted to escape from his cell at the Kansas City, Missouri, jail at midnight on May 2. He had pried loose an iron bar from a cot in his cell, and with this as a lever, he had worked loose one of the cell window's bars. The criminal was working on another window bar when he was caught. Nine days later he was taken to Butler, Missouri, to face the charge of being an accessory to the death of Constable Queen. Letters were found on Jones that indicated he was planning to blow up the Bates County Jail.[14]

On June 10, Shead's trial for murder began. Jones was charged with being his accomplice. The jury, with the exception of one carpenter, was made up entirely of farmers. A strong case against Shead was made by the

State, with the testimony of sixty-three witnesses, three of whom were doctors. The first prosecution witness was Constable Queen's widow. Two witnesses who were on the train car when Queen was killed were sure Shead did the shooting. Some witnesses reported that they had seen Shead and Jones drive and abandon a stolen car near Rich Hill, for the theft of which Jones was under arrest. One testified that Shead had told him Jones had been "pinched" in Hume. There were reports about the sales of stolen goods by the two criminals.

Other witnesses told of the whereabouts of the two criminals both before and after the murder. Three said they had seen Shead alone in Rich Hill that day. Seven other witnesses testified they saw Shead and Jones together around Rich Hill and Hume before Queen's murder. Shead was also seen in the company of Jones in different places in Kansas and Missouri after the shooting. Shead himself had said he was in St. Louis when the murder occurred.

Another seven witnesses were called for the defense. Two of them, eyewitnesses to the shooting, testified that Shead was not the man who did the shooting. According to Mary Coin of Rich Hill, Jones, wearing handcuffs, came to her house the night of the shooting with a man named Lewis. Cora Dixon, also of Rich Hill, talked about the reputation of the Lewis boys and their appearance in Rich Hill that same night. On June 12, Shead was found guilty of murder in the first degree and his punishment set at life imprisonment; Jones was acquitted of being an accomplice. Apparently car-theft charges were dropped.[15] Shead entered the Missouri state prison on June 20, 1914.[16]

CHAPTER 13:

"THE GIRL WITH THE AGATE EYES AND THE SMILE OF DEATH"

Newspapers referred to the beautiful blonde Mattie Howard as a "Golden Girl" and "the Queen of the Underworld." One of them called her "the Girl with the Agate Eyes and the Smile of Death"; it published ten pictures of men who, it said, were sweethearts of hers who had died.[1]

Mattie was born in the little railroad town of Preston, Idaho, to Charles and Martha E. Howard on November 11, 1894. The poor family of twelve children moved to Denver when Mattie was only nine months old. She spent a couple of years in a southern Colorado convent.[2] Afterward, living in Denver, she married Frank J. Landers, a retired Wyoming rancher.

Her brother Oliver was serving in the army, and one of his army friends was the tall and well-muscled Albert Pagle, a Brooklyn youth. The two soldiers robbed the Walsenburg, Colorado, post office. They were arrested and sentenced to time in the Leavenworth penitentiary. Howard left her husband for Pagle after his sentence ended. Pagle was also later convicted of car theft and served time in the Missouri state prison. After coming out of prison, Pagle robbed several post offices in the Kansas City region.[3]

Just before World War I, Mattie Howard left her family and moved to Kansas City, Missouri, where she joined Pagle and found employment at Montgomery Ward and Company during the day; at night she was on the switchboard at the Bell Telephone Company.[4]

Howard had many other criminal associates. On one occasion police went to arrest Dale Jones in a house in Kansas City, Missouri. Howard was with him when Jones escaped through a cellar door, but she told police she knew nothing. The crimes of Tony Cruye, a safecracker and highwayman, were also directed by Howard. She also linked up with Sam Taylor, an Indian bootlegger.[5] In 1921 a $500 dollar reward was offered for Howard's arrest. According to the reward notice:

> *Five Hundred Dollars reward will be paid by L. C. Talbot and Jesse E. James, bondmen, for the arrest or information leading to her arrest and the turning over to an officer of this department.*
>
> *She will be found with bank robbers, post office robbers and smugglers. Often goes out on the job dressed as a man and may be now disguised as such. She is a leader and planner of the most dangerous type. Would not hesitate to commit murder at any time. May now have her hair auburn or any other color. Natural color is dark blonde.*[6]

The reward notice also provided a description of Howard:

> *Name, Mattie Howard, No. 8639; /aliases of/ Mrs. Frank J. Vanders, M. N. Vanders, Mattie Davis, Marie Vanders; Crime, Invet. Susp. Murder; Age 23, Build M.; Weight 162, Height, 69.0…Eyes, Lt. Blue, Hair, Dk. Blonde; Complexion, Fair; Born, Preston, Idaho; Occupation, Telephone Opr.; Arrested, June 22, 1918. Remarks, Mole out cor. L eyebrow; mole back neck… Large, well shaped legs and good figure.*[7]

CHAPTER 14:

LOS ANGELES

Affter the trial of John Shead, Dale Jones was freed to return to stealing cars until the heat became too great in Missouri. He fled to Los Angeles in late 1914, where he committed many burglaries and stole numerous cars.[1] He was soon arrested for stealing an automobile. When Jones made an eloquent plea for mercy, the judge decided to give him another chance.

Within a week he was back before the same judge, who sentenced him to a short term in jail and declared he had a peculiar mania for stealing cars. Jones boasted that he had "an uncontrollable desire to steal motor cars that led him into forbidden paths."[2] Despite his criminal activities, a rich older woman took him into her home and cared for him.[3] "Kind, but misled persons" showered the youthful bandit with flowers while in jail and later effected his release on probation.[4]

While at the Los Angeles city jail, Jones met a shoplifter and store robber named Marie Celano (alias Marjie Dean), who had served time in a local institution.[5] Marie was born in New York City in 1898 to Peter and Camile Celano. The family had emigrated from Italy a few years before and later settled in Los Angeles. Very intelligent, Marie could speak

Spanish, Italian, and English.[6] Five feet one and five-eighths inches tall and weighing one hundred pounds, she had a slender build, an olive complexion, black hair, brown eyes, and pierced ears for earrings.[7]

According to a very inaccurate, fictional newspaper account:

> *She was born in Paris of degenerate stock among the social cesspools of that great city. Her father was a maker of spurious coins, that were passed on the tradesman by her mother, who had spent a part of her girlhood in the prison of Saint Lazare. The paternal grandfather of Margie /sic/ wore the ball and chain of the galleys at Toulon and her father was well acquainted with the insides of France, English and Italian prisons. Her parents emigrated to New York, where they resumed their activities in the counterfeiting line until the government ended their operation with long terms in the penitentiary.*
>
> *Margie /sic/ became a waif, a precocious waif, in the streets of New York. One dark and stormy night, a homeless, neglected and dejected creature sought shelter from the dismally howling wind and bitter cold in a doorway of New York's tenderloin district. That creature was Margie /sic/ Celano, or Margie /sic/ Dean. She was found there by Harry Longbaugh, alias the Sundance Kid, and by his wife, known in police records as Etta Place, two noted crooks of twenty years ago. They took her up and a few months later adopted her as their own*
>
> *Longbaugh and Etta Place belonged to the Butch Cassiday gang of burglars, holdup men and train robbers, whose headquarters were near Ft. Worth, Tex., but who operated in the west and northwest, and would hide away in New York and Syracuse until the excitement of their robberies had died down…*
>
> *It was in this atmosphere of robbery and crime that Margie /sic/ Dean grew up. She soon qualified as adept in thievery, and was known to the police of New York and Chicago as an expert "cold finger worker." The pseudonym in crookdom of a woman who steals*

diamonds. Caught in the act of robbing a Chicago jeweler, she was sent to Joliet Prison and there met Eva Lewis. At the expiration of her sentence Margie /sic/ went to Terre Haute [Indiana], where she was later joined by Eva Lewis and her husband, Frank Lewis. While on a visit from the west to his home at Sullivan [Indiana], Roy Sherrill stopped at Terre Haute with Dale Jones, who had been a Sherrill accomplice in a number of robberies. Jones fell violently in love with Margie /sic/ Dean, whom he met at the house of Frank and Eva Lewis, and they were married at Jeffersonville, Ind. The "best man" at their wedding was Roy Lancaster, alias Kansas City Blackie, a burglar and holdup man.[8]

Eva Lewis and Dean were too young to have been sent to Joliet, and there are no records of them from that prison.[9] Dean never knew Butch Cassiday and the Sundance Kid. Eva Lewis was the sister, not the wife of Frank Lewis.

Marie's father, Peter Celano, ran a winery near Azusa, California, until 1913. Hard times followed. Marie married a criminal named Charles Lynn, whom she later divorced. Dean's two sisters, Mary and Elizabeth, believed she must have been under the influence of the young Jones. They later said, "She was a home girl, and entirely different from what she is described to have been by the police. We all were raised in Los Angeles and grew up together. Never have we noticed any criminal tendencies in her."[10]

On June 16, 1915, Jones was arrested and charged with a holdup, burglary, and theft of an automobile. He was turned over to the Los Angeles County sheriff and released on probation.[11] Four months later, on October 21, Los Angeles detectives Hickok and Powell followed a stolen vehicle to a store in Los Angeles. Inside the car were Jones, the driver, and another thug. The two gangsters got into a fight with the proprietor of the place, Carl Keefer, when he accused them of selling stolen car parts. The detectives shot out of their car and ran to the store as the thugs were getting into their auto. Keefer jumped on the running board but was hit on the head by Jones and knocked to the ground. Meanwhile Powell was struck by a vehicle and his leg was broken. Hickok continued to give chase. Jones drove on the sidewalk until he crashed into a telephone pole. He drew a long knife and attempted to stab Hickok and two assisting officers until he was subdued.

The police photographed the criminal and published his picture in *The Detective*, a magazine with police circulation. After they read the magazine, officers in Kansas City, Missouri, demanded to get Jones for auto theft.[12] As they prepared to send Jones to Kansas City, Los Angeles policemen found in his hat a package of red pepper and in his shoes a number of fine steel saws, files, and steel springs, showing that he was planning an escape.[13] While he was being held in the Kansas City police headquarters, Jones tried to escape by burning a hole in the cell-room ceiling. Smelling the smoke, the jailer foiled the escape attempt.[14] In February 1916 Jones was sentenced to two years in the Missouri state prison. He was received at Jefferson City on February 27, 1916, and discharged on August 23, 1917.[15]

In 1917, soon after Jones's release, he, Sherrill, and Frank Lewis robbed an old man underneath a bridge in Kansas City, Missouri. Lewis struck the man on his head with a hammer and then searched him. When he found nothing of value, the criminal became angry. As they were leaving, Lewis turned to Sherrill and told him, "Roy, you go back there and hit that old man in the head again and bump him off proper." After Sherrill refused, a terrible argument ensued. Finally Lewis went back and attacked the man again. "I've bumped you off for good this time," he said. Sherrill fainted.[16]

On October 20, 1917, the gang went to the Missouri state prison to free Roy, Ora, and Shead, but Roy and Ora could not come for some unknown reason. After simply placing a ladder against the prison wall, Jones mounted it and dropped a rope for Shead to climb. While Shead climbed up the rope, Jones provided cover by firing two guns. When Shead reached the outside of the prison, Jones fired two more shots. They fled to a car driven by Frank Lewis and drove quickly away toward California and Mexico.[17]

Marjie Dean and Jones, both morphine addicts, went to horse races and played poker at Tijuana, Mexico. To prove how tough she was, Dean stole several hundred dollars and watches from a party of American sportsmen in broad daylight. To show what a crack pistol shot she was, Dean clipped the heads from Mexican quail.[18]

On December 8, 1917, Dale Jones; Dean's husband, Charles Lynn; and Dean's brother-in-law Ray Nieinever robbed the Culver City Commercial and Savings Bank in Culver City, California, at ten forty-five in the morning. More than $9,000 in gold and currency was taken. They somehow missed the just-delivered $35,000 payroll of the Triangle Motion Picture Studios. Dean was the getaway driver of a battered and dirty five-passenger Premier auto bearing a Washington state license plate. They were all armed with automatic pistols. The only person in the bank was cashier J. Bryant when the three male robbers entered. One of them, who was about six feet tall, dark, and shabbily dressed, asked for change for a five-dollar gold piece. After Bryant had gotten the change, the robbers pointed their guns at him and forced him to enter the vault and lie down. One robber kept watch over him while the others grabbed money and gold from the vault and cash drawer.

After leaving the bank, the robbers held up three men from Triangle Studios who were passing by and stole $176 and their watches. The outlaws then hurried to their auto, and Dean drove them away. Fifteen minutes later, the chief of police, captain of detectives, five officers, and county sheriff reached the bank, but found no clues. Burns Detective Agency operatives tried to get fingerprints and other evidence, but were also not successful. More than fifty city and county officers searched for the robbers. Motorcycle policemen set up roadblocks. The bandits' car was seen going past Triangle Studios at seventy miles an hour, but no traces of the robbers were later found. The bank was fully covered by insurance.[19]

CHAPTER 15:

MORE BANK ROBBERIES

The gang decided to rob several banks during 1918. To show how easy bank robberies were, Frank Lewis claimed that at an unstated date, he had robbed a bank at Cement City, Kansas, by himself, armed only with a toy pistol. Although hoping for $28,000, he still grabbed a generous $6,000. It was used for the legal defense of his brothers.[1]

On February 4, 1918, the unmasked Jones entered the Quindaro State Bank at Kansas City, Kansas, just after three in the afternoon as cashier Frank L. McGonigle was making up the daily report and putting $2,800 into the vault. Frank Lewis, smoking a cigar, and Kansas City Blackie (Lancaster) stood guard outside. Bank bookkeeper Beatrice Gilliford was the only other person inside. The robber threw a counterfeit half-dollar on the counter and asked what the cashier would give for it. "Nothing," McGonigle responded. Jones pulled out a revolver. "What'll you give for this? Fork over the cash, quick!" he demanded.

With one hand McGonigle gave the bandit a roll of $2,000. With the other he swept additional piles of money to one side where they would not likely be seen. Jones ran out of the bank and escaped with his partners-in-crime, with Lewis driving. They proceeded through the town.[2] On Main Street, within a block of the city hall, they passed a police car. Meanwhile policemen were wandering down in the willows by the Missouri River looking for two men seen running toward the river.[3]

Eight days later, on Wednesday, February 12, assistant cashier Clare Johnston was sitting at his desk at the South Side Bank in Kansas City, Missouri, about 2:25 p.m., just before closing time, when Jones alone entered. The well-dressed bandit wore a dark suit, a light checkered overcoat, a dark hat, and a large pair of black-rimmed glasses. He had a large and very black mustache, but it did not look real. Jones walked up to the cashier's window. "Well, how is business?" he inquired.

"Pretty good," answered Johnston.

"Well, it's been bad with me, so put up your hands, and be quick about it," the bandit quietly commanded as he pulled out a revolver.

Showing no evidence of nervousness, Jones worked with quiet precision. When the criminal told Johnston to open the door to the steel vault, the assistant cashier told him he did not know the combination. In fact the door was ajar. Stenographer Mary Laughlin, working at her typewriter while the holdup was in progress, was forced to enter a closet with Johnston. Before closing the closet door, the robber went behind the partition and began filling his pockets with packages of ten- and twenty-dollar bills.

A fifteen-year-old boy named George Strom then entered to get change. Startled at seeing a strange man behind the partition, the boy headed for the door.

"Just a moment, please," yelled the bandit, pointing his revolver at the boy. "You are young and might tell something." When the robber turned to cover the boy with his revolver, Johnston reached out of the closet and turned the combination, locking the vault door. The boy was then also forced into the closet, and Jones locked it.

After grabbing $4,400, Jones ran through the rear door. Several hundred dollars in paper money was left lying on the counter. Johnston climbed out of the closet (which was not enclosed at the top) and called the police. When they arrived five minutes later, nearby streets were combed, but there was no trace of the bandit. The bank, fully covered by burglary insurance, had just opened January 23. Officers believed the robber was the same man who had committed the Quindaro robbery on February 4.[4]

On March 14, 1918, Shead was captured when he got drunk and fought with police in California; he was returned to the Missouri state prison.[5] Two months later, on May 4, Jones and Dean were married at San Bernandino, California.[6]

Jones and Kansas City Blackie, without Frank Lewis, robbed the State Bank of Sugar Creek in Sugar Creek, Missouri, on May 25. The two young outlaws were dressed in khaki clothing; Jones had a light, thin mustache and wore a long, tan raincoat. They jumped from a brown Hudson roadster parked in front of the bank shortly before ten in the morning, left the engine on, and entered the building. Jones tendered a ten-dollar bill to bank president J. C. Gant, who was standing behind the counter.

"Change for a ten, please," Jones said. Both outlaws then drew revolvers and covered him and two women clerks, the only ones in the bank. Jones ordered Gant, "Lie down!" The bank president dropped behind the counter. The two women were forced into a vault, and the door was closed. About $1,200 was grabbed, which the bandits put in their pockets. A sack marked "5,000" that contained five thousand pennies was taken, perhaps because they believed it contained $5,000 in gold. About $4,000 was left in the vault. After the bandits fled, Gant arose from the floor and called the police. Posses of Sugar Creek citizens in cars tried to pursue the bandits, but soon lost them.[7]

Meanwhile, Ora Lewis appealed his murder conviction to the Missouri Supreme Court, which affirmed his death sentence on February 18, 1918. The execution was set for April 5. During her popular nightclub act in St. Louis, Ora's sister Eva was busy soliciting thousands of signatures on a petition for executive clemency for him. Many wanted to see the sister of the notorious Lewis boys. Several times Eva visited the state executive mansion. In fact she waited so long for the governor, she contracted pneumonia and was hospitalized for several weeks. On April 3, two days before the execution date, Governor Frederick D. Gardner commuted Ora's sentence to life imprisonment.[8]

THE SPANISH FLU

The influenza epidemic of 1918–19 killed somewhere between twenty million and forty million people, more deaths than among soldiers in World War I. It was the worst epidemic in recorded history. More people died in one year of influenza than in the "Black Death" of the Middle Ages. Twenty percent of the world's population was infected.[9] It was especially deadly for people between the ages of twenty and forty, a very productive segment of society. As early as the spring of 1918, the influenza appeared in Kansas and in military camps throughout the United States. Perhaps 43,000 US soldiers perished from the disease, about the same number that were killed in combat. The "Spanish Flu" infected 28 percent of Americans, and 675,000 of them died. Most deaths occurred between August and November 1918.[10] It ended quickly, but there was a minor repeat of the epidemic in March 1919. "Fire and brimstone" preachers screamed that such death was God's punishment for a sinful people.[11] To stop the spread of the virus, many towns closed such public places as theaters, schools, saloons, churches, and public meeting houses.[12] According to one writer, "There's nothing more frightening than a killer no one sees, and that no one seems able to stop."[13]

CHAPTER 16:

MURDER OF A DIAMOND KING

On May 24, 1918, Jones, dressed as a woman, along with Sam Taylor, Mattie Howard, and fifty-year-old Joseph Morino, an importer of fine jewelry known as a diamond "king" said to be worth almost a quarter of a million dollars, had a party in Kansas City, Missouri.[1] The two "women"—one his "sweetheart"—had lured Morino into apartment 301, a tiny three-room kitchenette apartment at the Touraine Apartment Hotel. With thick and soundproof walls, the recently built apartments were in a quiet section of Kansas City, where people could come and go and not be paid any attention.

The female night clerk saw a couple come to the hotel desk shortly after seven in the evening to get their room key. Another heavyset "woman" (i.e., Jones) and the unseen Taylor was with them. In the apartment, one of the men pointed a revolver at Morino and asked for his money.[2] They demanded a check, signed by him and made payable to bearer. Until the check was cashed, the jeweler would be kept prisoner.[3]

Morino's hands were bound to a bedpost. Feeling sorry for him, Howard loosened the baling wire that encircled his wrists and inserted a towel between the cutting strands so the flesh would not be torn. After he squirmed and managed to free his arms, Howard struck him several times on the head with a blackjack. Although stunned, Morino jumped to his feet and tried to get to the hall door, but fell a few feet from it. The criminals went through his pockets and found a big roll of bills. On his fingers were rings valued at more than $2,000. Afraid the jeweler would tell who robbed him, they decided to kill him. Jones or Taylor used the butt end of a revolver to crush his skull by a few blows to the unconscious man's forehead. They closed the hall door and left. The group was not seen to leave the very quiet room. How the murderers left without being seen was a mystery. One theory was that they used the fire escape.[4]

Early the next morning, a taxicab driver picked up a man and two women from the Touraine Apartment, took the women to one hotel, and left the man at another hotel. The driver later told police he got a good look at his passengers and identified the man as Sam Taylor and one of the women as Mattie Howard. He did not know the identity of the second woman.[5]

A porter entered the apartment with a passkey just before 11 a.m. when his knock was unanswered, and saw much disorder. A table and bureau were close together and chairs were overturned, but the small kitchenette was undisturbed. Blood covered the floor, walls, furniture, and window curtains. The fully dressed Morino was found dead near the hall door. Baling wire still encircled Morino's right hand. His hat and two blood-covered hairpins lay near his body. An empty whiskey bottle indicAted Morino was drunk when he was killed. In his pockets was found a check with Mattie Howard's name on it.[6]

City detective Harry Arthur believed that the women were merely decoys and the actual crime was committed by a man.[7] "It is terrible," Mrs. Morino murmured the day after the murder. "My poor, dear husband. He was so good and kind to me. No, he didn't stay away nights—much. No, I never suspected another woman—we had been married thirty years."[8]

Three days later the identities of the murderers were established, but the twenty-three-year-old blonde woman had fled the city. Howard fit the description of the blonde woman seen with Morino—blonde, rather heavyset, young, and attractive.[9] She was arrested with Sam Taylor on June 22 at Raton, New Mexico, but later jumped her bond.[10]

The investigation revealed that Howard had first met Morino early in April when she bought a watch at his pawnshop. On April 30, at a restaurant near the pawnshop, she tried to cash a ten-dollar check, but was refused. She then went to the pawnshop. At first the wealthy jeweler refused, but later he accepted a check for one hundred dollars. The check bounced, but he forgave her and continued to see her. For the next six weeks, she called Morino frequently, and they had many night meetings, although it was difficult for him to get away from his "home loving" wife.[11]

Two days before the murder, at about noon, Morino, carrying a black suitcase, and dressed in a white silk-waist shirt and a trim, light straw hat, approached the hotel lobby desk with a young woman and was given keys to room number 301. The hotel manager and a black hotel employee escorted the couple to their room.

"What do you think of the spot, dear?" asked the woman. "You're the one to be pleased," Morino replied. She laughed and said, "It sure is all right with me." The woman signed the register, "B. Stanley and wife, Detroit," paying a week's rent of twelve dollars. "Mrs. Stanley" and the older man left the hotel with her arm through his.[12] "My husband and I will be back soon," she cheerily remarked.[13]

That night Morino and his real wife went to the theater. The next afternoon Mrs. Morino visited him in his store—the last time she saw him alive. Very busy that day, Morino decided to close earlier than usual. His chief clerk answered the telephone at eight that night; a woman asked for "Joe." Morino came to the phone and smiled. "I'll meet you at nine fifteen," he said. The next evening he was murdered.[14]

On June 29, 1918, the Industrial State Bank of Argentine in Kansas City, Kansas, was robbed at noon by Frank Lewis, Jones, Kansas City Blackie, and Sherrill. There was less cash than usual because of the cashing of paychecks. Only two women employees were in the bank. Sherrill guarded the front door, and Lewis stayed in a stolen car, while Blackie and Jones entered. Bank clerk Lora Campbell screamed when she saw Lancaster point a revolver at assistant cashier Lena Boeke. Jones pushed Campbell to the floor and stifled her screams. She begged him to release her, promising not to scream. He forced her to open the vault door. After Sherrill kept one of the women from running out the door and yelling, he entered the bank to help gather up the money on the counters and in the vault. The bandits tried to force the women into the vault, but the vault door would not close. They warned them to remain in the vault for ten minutes, but the women gave the alarm immediately after the robbers left.

The trio of robbers fled the bank with $2,305, joined Lewis in the auto, and drove rapidly away. It was not until an hour and a quarter later that detectives left police headquarters to investigate.[15] Lewis and Jones told Sherrill they got only a few dollars and gave him only $14 for his share. Sherrill later said, "I understand that we got nearly $4,000 from that bank and I sure was sore about the division."[16]

CHAPTER 17:

TRAIN ROBBERY

On July 10, 1918, thirteen masked bandits held up the "Texas Special" of the Missouri, Kansas & Texas Railway—"Katy" train No. 27—and shot several train employees and passengers at Koch siding, four miles south of Paola, Kansas. The train ran between Kansas City and Parsons, Kansas, connecting there with the through-Texas train that ran between St. Louis and San Antonio. The robbery was carefully planned by those who knew a lot about the train schedule. They believed it had expensive cargo. However, large amounts of money never were shipped on the No. 27.

The "Texas Special" left Kansas City at 9:15 p.m.[1] At 10:30 p.m. the train took the "blind siding" at Koch to let a northbound train to pass. After the main line was clear, two outlaws went over to the engine tender and began firing—the signal for a fusillade by gang members. Several armed and masked men emerged from the darkness.

Two of them had the job of taking care of the engineer and fireman.[2] "Put up your hands," they ordered.[3] Two other bandits went to the mail car and seized four packages of registered mail. Gang members also entered the baggage car. Express messenger W. Nimon, alone in the express car, was forced to come out by two bandits who ordered him, "Come down or I'll bring you down." Several shots were fired at Nimon when he did not move fast enough for them. The express safe was removed.[4]

In only three minutes, the fireman, engineer, express agent, and railway mail clerks were ordered to go into the first passenger coach and lie down in the narrow space between seats or on the seats themselves. Going up and down the aisle, the bandits yelled orders and fired shots into the roof and floor of the car. When J. E. Williams, a porter, tried to escape through a window, he was shot in the hip. Although fireman R. E. Caster lay facedown on a seat with his feet a few inches into the aisle, he was shot in one foot and the left thigh. Train auditor C. T. Witcher, after hearing shots fired, hurried into the express car to see what was happening; he was shot at several times. As Witcher reached for his pistol, he was hit in his left ankle. Slightly injured, he was knocked down after a bullet struck a change pocket. Meanwhile, the engineer and fireman were also shot when they resisted the outlaws' commands.[5]

One robber ordered the passengers to hand over their money and jewelry, but Mrs. L. D. Williams, a passenger from Achille, Oklahoma, refused to obey the command. The robber, his face obscured by a large handkerchief and a slouch hat that came well down over his face, exclaimed, "Take that, then!" A bullet entered her left shoulder and lodged in her lung. She was the most severely wounded. Although it was mostly quiet after that, four bandits still fired occasional shots.[6]

Brakeman Jake Darkes was threatened by the robbers. "Don't shoot him—don't you know that man is Jake Darkes," one of the robbers said to another.[7]

The engineer was forced to decouple the mail and express cars and back them down the main line about one and one-fourth miles. A signal was given by a bandit in the engine.[8] Meanwhile the bandits in the coach fled and fired about seventy revolver shots at the windows as they ran along both sides of the train; curses punctuated the shooting.

Pullman conductor R. E. Cowan reached up with his left hand to extinguish the lights in the sleepers in order to protect passengers from the bandits. But before he could touch the switch, he heard a warning. A rifle shot shattered a window and a piece of flying glass cut an ugly gash over Cowan's right eye. He did not try again to turn off the lights.[9]

Muskogee businessman J. D. Murray, a passenger in the smoker, was impressed by the well-organized robbers. He later said:

> *The crew of bandits was well-organized, each man having been given a number by which he was directed by the leader. I heard numbers called as high as twelve, but saw only six men. Man "no. 6" was called upon to do the most work. The man who stood front platform after the engine and baggage car had been taken away was a young fellow and I think without doubt I could identify him. When he took the platform he said, "I am going to give you fellows some Jesse James stuff," and he proceeded to fire down the aisle. Three shots passed very close to me, one passing just an inch or so in front of my face.*
>
> *All the bandits seemed to be very young, in their twenties....There was a great deal of confusion on the train, in fact every time a shot was fired, and about one hundred were fired, I think some would scream and others pray. From their actions I would say most of the bandits were or had been railroad men.*[10]

The robbers ran to a Cadillac Phaeton driven by the small, dark-haired Dean, and another car on a nearby highway. As the robbers were transferring their loot to the vehicles, a freight train arrived. Two shots were fired at it.[11] "Come on, boys, let's go," one of them shouted.[12] They headed into the night toward Kansas City, about forty-six miles away.

Many footprints and tracks of a car were found near where the vehicles had been. One of the footprints was of an abnormally large foot. The wounded were taken to a hospital. A posse of two hundred and fifty men scoured the countryside for three days and then gave up the hunt. Two men were arrested, but soon released.

American Express Company officials reported that only a small safe containing about $199 in money and jewelry was stolen.[13] Government investigators later told Sherrill that only $15 had been taken. Hundreds of dollars may have been stolen from train passengers. Much mail was taken, but it was unknown if there was any money or valuables in the mail.[14] Others falsely claimed the robbers had made a big haul. Two days later a train safe, blasted open with nitroglycerin, was found near Paola. It was reported that about $50,000 had been removed. After that, US Marines were put on every mail train in the country.[15]

CHAPTER 18:

DARING ESCAPES

During the summer of 1918, members of the Lewis-Jones gang…, lived in a quiet residential district of Kansas City, Missouri. Moving about openly, they were expensively dressed and drove the best high-powered autos. About June 1, Frank Lewis, pretending to be a livestock dealer from Wichita named Harry Clayton; his wife, Bessie; and six-month-old baby boy, Bobbie, rented a house at 3715 Wyandotte Street. His references were not checked.

Lewis was arrested twice for speeding. The first time he paid a two-dollar fine in court, and the second time he forfeited an eleven-dollar bond.

On July 8, Dale Jones rented a house nearby. The outlaw told neighbors he had been married only a month to Dean. The secretive Jones kept the blinds drawn, but he moved about town openly, even selling a motorcycle to a motorcycle policeman and going to the Woodland Avenue police station to get paid. Lewis frequently visited Jones's place, always arriving in his vehicle.[1]

Jones, Frank, Kansas City Blackie, Blackie's brother Harry Lancaster, Frank Knight, and Roy Sherrill left Kansas City in three cars and headed on mostly dirt roads toward the state prison at Jefferson City, Missouri, with plans to free Roy, Ora, and Shead on July 11. Each car had two gangsters and guns. The last three days had been hot and rainy. For hours the gangsters tried to get through the mud, but fifteen miles east of Sedalia and still forty-five miles from the prison, they had to give up and turn back. The gang did not know that more than a hundred citizens and guards were waiting for them. They had been alerted by Eva's visit to her brothers in the prison visitors' room a week before that had been recorded by a Dictaphone.[2]

Back in Kansas City, Missouri, in the early morning darkness of July 16, four police officers saw two bright lights go on and off in a speeding car, and they followed it. "Stop," yelled the officers. The vehicle picked up speed. Eight blocks away, four Lewis-Jones gang members stopped, jumped from the darkened vehicle, and ran into a nearby field. When the police arrived, the bandits fired at them. Police returned the gunfire, but it was ineffective. More than twenty-five revolver shots were exchanged. The hood and side of the police vehicle were hit; two tires were flattened. The gangsters leaped into their car and escaped, while the officers returned to the police station in a damaged vehicle.[3]

Two days later an informer told County Marshal Harvey Hoffman that Frank Lewis and Dale Jones were hiding at a house in the city. Hoffman did not find the two criminals there, but discovered four females: Frank's wife, sixteen-year-old Bessie Clayton; Dean; Bessie's mother, Mrs. Fanny Rogers; and another daughter of Mrs. Rogers, ten-year-old Gertrude.

Hoffman and four city detectives hid in the house all day. The nervous women were not allowed to answer several phone calls. At 9:20 p.m., a car with Lewis and Jones and two other gangsters was heard coming into the yard. Knowing the criminals were on guard because of the unanswered phone calls, a detective named Carroll went out to prevent the criminals from going into the garage, where it would be more difficult to arrest them. Immediately after turning a spotlight on Carroll, the bandits opened fire. Although temporarily blinded by the light, Carroll returned the fire with two revolvers. Officers in the house, recognizing Lewis and

Jones, shot at them as the gangsters backed up and sped away. One of the criminals was thought to have been hit. Across the street a woman saw one gangster fall from his seat when the car started to move. Nobody else was hurt.[4]

The next day, on July 19, police searched the Lewis house and arrested the three women there. Mrs. Roger's daughter, Gertrude, was taken along. About four hundred dollars' worth of jewelry and a derby hat believed to belong to one of the train robbers was found. Special agents for the railroad and Wells Fargo verified that the jewelry came from the train safe. Police also found several unusual bullets of the type used by the outlaws at the train holdup site and the gunfights on July 16 and July 18.

Bessie Clayton and Dean identified the pictures of the men, but denied they knew anything about the train robbery or the whereabouts of the men. Postal inspectors also questioned the women, who admitted Lewis and Jones had been living in the house. Bessie said she had married Lewis two weeks before, after she had arrived from Los Angeles.[5]

Early that night Jones called police headquarters to tell them the entire thirteen-member gang was coming to "get" their women. An emergency squad with riot guns was set up at police headquarters. When a riot gun was accidentally fired, about twenty officers ran toward the location of the shooting, believing the gangsters had come, but they never did. The women were released a few days later. Detectives had seen Jones in city saloons, but each time he always left before being positively identified.[6]

THE KANSAS CITY UNDERWORLD

The dominant gang in Kansas City, Missouri, was the Kansas City Black Hand, led by James Balestrere; it came to later be called the Balestrere Gang. Balestrere had moved to Milwaukee, Wisconsin, from Sicily in 1903. Five years later he was in Kansas City and had a close relationship with political boss Thomas Pendergrast. Soon authorities considered him to be the most powerful underworld figure west of Chicago. By 1912, Balestrere had established control of criminal activities in Kansas City.

That year Joseph DiGiovanni, wanted for several murders in his native Palermo, Sicily, appeared in Kansas City. There were rumors several Mafia bosses in Sicily had sent him to that city. His brother Peter was already there and both were members of the Balestrere Gang. The brothers stole from and extorted local merchants, largely Italian immigrants. Their chief enforcer was Paul Cantanzano. In 1915, the city's Italian community had finally had enough and took action against him. About twenty local businessmen filed charges against the brothers, and Kansas City police detective Louis Olivero arrested them. However, the brothers had no fear of the police. Before a trial began, Olivero was discovered shot dead.[7]

CHAPTER 19:

BANK ROBBERY IN INDIANAPOLIS

On August 8, 1918, Lewis, Lancaster, Jones, and Dean robbed the South Side Bank in Indianapolis. The unmasked gangsters parked in front of the bank and entered it at noon with drawn revolvers. Dean was at the wheel of a low, underslung, high-powered, five-passenger gray Hudson with an Iowa license tag. Inside the bank were its president, John W. Lauch, and bank employees L. A. Wiles and Lenora Brockman.[1] "Throw up your hands," ordered the bandits.[2] Lewis jumped over the gate to the bank interior and struck Lauch on the head with a revolver butt, knocking him unconscious.

According to Lauch, "I did not realize what was happening until I saw one of the three men who came in the door hurdle the gate leading into the interior of the bank. I saw he had a revolver, and when he ordered me to throw up my hands I tried to obey as quickly as possible. He then struck me on the head with the weapon. I was seated at my desk and had just started to get up when he struck me."[3]

The other two bandits made the bank employees enter the cashier's cage and lie flat on the floor. They gathered up the cash, while Lewis guarded the employees. Meanwhile, John A. Herman, manager of the Union Street Wire Company, entered the bank. One of the robbers struck Herman on the head, knocking him down before he had time to realize what was going on, and dragged him into the cashier's cage with the bank employees.

The gangsters drove rapidly away with $8,380 in cash and $10,000 in five- and ten-dollar gold pieces. George Nathan passed the bank with a horse and wagon and saw the bandits climb into a car and rapidly drive away. Believing they were bank robbers, Nathan pursued but soon lost sight of them.[4] "They went so fast after turning onto Union Street that I couldn't see 'em for the dust," Nathan told the police.[5]

At a nearby garage, the bandits switched to a stolen black Packard. A motorcycle policeman and a police squad with riot guns chased after the fugitives but could not find them. Police in nearby towns were notified to be on the lookout for them and patrolled all nearby roads, but they could not find any trace of the gang and had no idea who they were. Lauch, not hurt seriously, was treated by a doctor.[6] The robbery was called "one of the boldest committed in Indianapolis in several years."[7]

The Pinkertons investigated the robbery and discovered that the female driver of the getaway car matched the description of someone who had opened an account at the bank under the name of Irene Brown several weeks earlier. A few days before the robbery, she had withdrawn her entire balance. Agents canvassed the neighborhood of the address she had given and located the stolen Hudson getaway car, but no fingerprints were found. In the vehicle were woman's clothes: a hat, veil, dress, and shoes with the label of a Kansas City department store. The clothes were very large for a woman, which led to the belief that it might have been a disguise for a man. A garage owner told the detectives a young couple had parked a Packard in his garage for a month. The girl answered to the description of "Irene Brown." The man fit the description of Dale Jones: light complexioned and blue-eyed, with the tip of the middle finger of his right hand missing. The Pinkertons' Kansas City office checked with local lawmen, who were aware of a cross-dressing criminal named Dale Jones.

The detective agency was the first organization to have linked the gang to several bank robberies, as well as to the train robbery. Descriptions of the robbers were similar in all of the crimes.

Pinkerton undercover operatives—from out of town so they would not be recognized—drove taxis and picked up fares near underworld establishments. Sometimes they would get useful intelligence from talkative or drunken passengers. Other Pinkerton men had jobs as waiters and bartenders in criminal dives. They even found that Jones wore a size seven-and-a-half shoe—the same measurement as that of the women's footwear found in the abandoned vehicle in Indianapolis.[8]

Additional clues came from Dale Jones's attempted robbery on August 12 of forty-five-year-old cab driver David Wolf at Terre Haute, Indiana. The bandit had hired Wolf to take him to the country club east of the city to meet Margie Dean late that evening. She wasn't at the club, and at about eleven o'clock, the criminal told Wolf to drive him back to the city. On the way, Jones ordered Wolf to turn off the main road onto a dark side road.

When the cab driver refused, Jones threatened him and hit Wolf over the head with a revolver butt. As Wolf grabbed a piece of iron, the bandit shot him in the back, with the bullet passing through his body and touching the lobe of his heart. Although seriously wounded, Wolf fought with the gangster and seized his revolver. When another car approached, the frightened Jones jumped from the cab, leaving a briefcase in the car. Despite bleeding freely, Wolf drove to a former roadhouse near the Vigo County fairgrounds, where he collapsed on the floor. He was taken to St. Anthony's Hospital, but there was little hope he would survive. The next day, however, Wolf slightly improved and soon made a miraculous recovery.[9]

Jones had left behind three hundred dollars in bills in his briefcase. Some packages containing fifty dollars each were bound with South Side State Bank wrappers. Clothes bearing the name of the Plymouth Clothing Company of Quincy, Illinois, were also found. Employees there gave the

Pinkertons descriptions of three men who matched the descriptions of Lewis, Jones, and Lancaster.[10]

Three suspicious men and a well-dressed woman had registered at a local hotel on August 11. They were lavish in their tips, posed as United States Secret Service agents, and disappeared after Wolf was assailed. Two of the men and the woman had offered a taxi driver thirty dollars to leave the city. No trace of them was found.[11]

Wolf afterward identified the photograph of Roy Sherrill as that of the man who shot him, but H. C. Webster, chief of the Webster Detective Agency, who worked on the case for the Indiana Bankers Association, believed that Wolf was wrong in his identification—that it was Jones and not Sherrill who shot Wolf.[12]

A massive manhunt for the Lewis-Jones gang included the Pinkertons; Burns detectives; federal agents; and state, county, and city police.[13]

CHAPTER 20:
A TRIP TO DENVER

Frank and Eva had strong feelings for their mother and stepfather, so the Pinkertons kept under constant surveillance the Bubb house on Wyandotte Avenue, in Kansas City, Missouri, which was surrounded by vacant lots and heavy underbrush. On September 6, 1918, the Bubbs sent two trunks to Union Station, left their house, and visited several neighbors to say good-bye.

At the station a Pinkerton agent standing in the same ticket line as the couple bought a ticket he was not planning to use. He heard Mr. Bubb asking for two fares to Denver. Pinkerton agents discovered that their two trunks were put on the Denver train, and they obtained the stub numbers. They wired a report on what they had found to their Denver office. At first, agents were not sure that following the couple would lead to members of the Lewis-Jones gang. However, neighbors had told the agents that the Bubbs had told them they were going to Chicago—not Denver. This suggested the gang was going to Denver.[1]

Meanwhile Kansas City, Missouri, Chief of Detectives I. B. Walston received several anonymous telephone calls that falsely told him of Dale Jones's location. Each call was taken seriously and police cars were sent to various places, but nothing was found. On the evening of September 6, a woman speaking Spanish made an annoying call to Walston, who did not speak Spanish. She finally said in English, "Hold the line, Ike [Walston's nickname]."

A man who also spoke Spanish got on the telephone. "What is this, anyway?" Walston asked.

"Ike, you've been getting a lot of tips on that Dale Jones fellow lately, haven't you? Don't bother to answer, because I'll tell you what the tips were."

The caller went on to mention details of the recent false reports on Jones. The chief of detectives suddenly realized he was talking to the criminal himself. He signaled to an officer to trace the call.

"It won't do you any good to trace this call, Ike, for I've got things timed in such a way that Marjie and me will be out of this drugstore before anybody can get here," Jones said. "But don't let that bother you, Ike," Jones continued, "for I'm ready to give myself up. In case you haven't guessed, this is Dale Jones calling, and I'll be at the Bubb house on Wyandotte Avenue. You know the number; you've been shadowing it long enough."[2]

Detectives went to the drugstore where Jones had made the call, but Jones and Dean were gone. Walston believed Jones was truly planning to surrender. Eight of Walston's best detectives went to the Bubb house, where they saw lights inside. They were fired upon from both sides of the property. After dropping to the ground, the detectives returned the gunfire. A street lamp casting light on the policemen made them sitting ducks, while at least six criminals were safe because they kept moving and were not visible in the bushes and darkness.

The officers could tell gangsters were moving backward, for their gun flashes became farther away. Finally their firing stopped. Amazingly, the detectives escaped injury. As a car drove away, they heard laughter. After the chief of detectives had received a phone call about the ambush, he got another call from Jones. "This is Dale Jones again, Ike. What did you think of that little party we just staged? I guess that'll teach you a thing or two!" Laughing, he finished by saying, "The next thing on the program is that we're going to swipe a car. This Packard we're running around in has got too hot."[3]

Later that night, the gangsters in the Packard forced prominent Kansas City citizen George T. Cook to take his Marmon car to the curb near his home on the outskirts of the city. They seized the vehicle and drove Cook out of Kansas City to an isolated road, where they bound and gagged him and robbed him of sixty dollars and jewelry. After he managed to free himself, he walked until he found a phone to call the police, at around midnight.

Since the Marmon had only enough gasoline to go about ten miles, the lawmen decided the gangsters probably had to have stopped at a gas station nearby. The next morning they found the station on the outskirts of the city. An attendant reported that four men, two women, and a baby in a Marmon that matched the description of Cook's car had come there for gas and oil and to have the tires checked. He had become alarmed when he saw the muzzles of two shotguns in the back of the vehicle. Photos of Lewis, Sherrill, Lancaster, and the wives of Jones and Lewis were identified, and the description of the fourth man fit that of Dale Jones.

"Did anyone in the car indicate where the party was going?" asked a Pinkerton agent. "Yes," the attendant replied, "they wanted to know the best route to Colorado, and I told them. I heard one of the girls in the back saying to the other that Denver would be a good place for the baby."[4]

Since Pinkerton officials believed the Bubbs would get off their train at the Denver depot, where a Pinkerton agent could pick up their trail, no agent was put on the train with the couple. However, Denver agent Joseph F. Miller did not see the couple or their baggage at the Denver depot. Miller learned from questioning the crew that the Bubbs had left the train at a stop outside Denver, and a truck had come for them. The trail was then lost.

No sightings of the gangsters or the stolen Marmon had been reported anywhere between Kansas City and Denver in the previous two days. If the Bubb couple could be found, the gangsters could also be discovered. Agents checked out the local rooming houses. The landlady of a rooming house at 808 East Eighteenth Avenue told Miller that a couple who matched the description of John and Martha Bubb, using the name of Simpson, had rented a room the same day the train had arrived.

The detective searched their room when they were out and discovered ticket stubs for trunks that had the same numbers as the trunks owned by the couple. Just after Miller left the room, the couple returned. The detective remained in the rooming house. Soon Mr. Bubb went to the first floor and used a public telephone.

Miller, on the stairs, heard him calling a number, but could not listen to the phone conversation because someone came down the stairs. Nevertheless he was able to learn the phone number called. A checkup revealed the call was from the lobby of an apartment house only a block away.

The apartment house superintendent told the officers that the day before, two men and a young woman had rented an apartment. One of the men and the girl had said their names were Forbes, and they claimed to be married. The other man, name unknown, was supposed to be the couple's friend. The trio matched the descriptions of Jones, Dean, and Kansas City Blackie. A search of the gang's apartment discovered an important clue—a distinctive, uncommon, and expensive perfume on a woman's handkerchief on a table, apparently belonging to Marjie Dean.

Meanwhile, an operative was placed in a room across the hall from the Bubbs. Though a crack in the door of his room, the agent soon saw Lewis and Jones, dressed as a woman, going into the couple's room for short visits. The detective could tell "she" was a man masquerading as a woman because of Jones's large feet.

Lawmen knew the gang was in two groups, one being Jones, Dean, and Lancaster, with Sherrill, Lewis, and his wife and their baby staying elsewhere. If the Bubbs were kept under surveillance, it was believed all the gangsters could be located and arrested.

One time, the suspicious Jones left the rooming house, but the Pinkerton detective decided not to follow. He did flash a signal from a window to another agent stationed across the street, but the agents did not see Jones leave the building. After ten minutes they realized Jones must have gone out the backdoor.[5]

CHAPTER 21:

"THE WILDEST NIGHT"

Two days later, on the morning of September 13, 1918, Agent Miller followed two cars from Denver to Colorado Springs, Colorado. Riding in a Marmon were Jones, wearing a black suit and hat; Dean, wearing a brown dress; and Kansas City Blackie, also wearing a black suit and hat. The other car carried Frank, Eva, Sherrill, and a new gang member, twenty-year-old George Eudaley (alias Ray Long).[1]

Fresh out of the Missouri state prison on August 20, Eudaley had served a two-year sentence for assault and robbery. Born in Kentucky, he was five feet eight and a half inches tall, with medium-black hair, blue eyes, and a medium-sallow complexion. Eudaley had previously worked as a professional chauffeur.[2] Missing from the group were Harry Lancaster and Frank Knight, both dismissed as gang members because they were considered too cowardly.

Just before getting to Colorado Springs, sensing that they were being followed, the gangsters—who were planning to rob two banks in that city—stopped their cars, pretending to have motor trouble. Detective

Miller drove past them. He waited for them while he had lunch at Palmer Lake, twenty-five miles north of the city. Seeing the gangsters go by, he called the Colorado Springs police.

Lewis decided that a detective following them and possibly alerting the police force in Colorado Springs did not make for a good day for a bank robbery. He turned the car around and went back to Denver. Jones, Lancaster, and Dean were not so easily deterred. They continued on to Colorado Springs.[3]

According to two employees of the Vreeland Filling Station, Frank Henderson and Roy Settle:

> *We were busy working with a Hudson car that had driven into the station [by an elderly woman] for oil and gas. Settle was filling the radiator and I was pouring oil into the engine, when the Marmon car drove up. We recognized it at once from the description we had and also by the license tag. Henderson went into the office and telephoned the police headquarters while Settle killed as much time as possible tinkering about the Hudson so the police officers would have time to arrive and make the arrests.*
>
> *Jones was driving the Marmon car and stopped just behind the Hudson. He got out, unscrewed the cap from the radiator and started filling it with water."*[4]

Chief of Detectives John Rowan took Henderson's call. According to the local newspaper:

> *For 14 years "Johnny" Rowan was a peace officer in Colorado. He helped to keep order in Colorado City when that community was in its wildest days. He was a special agent on the Denver and Rio Grande railroad and went through a series of dangerous experiences throughout which he established and maintained a reputation for coolness and daring seldom equaled in the west. For several years he has been chief of detectives on the local force and was noted for the uncanny judgment he exercised in running down difficult cases.*[5]

Eight officers in two cars set out for the gas station. Detectives Rowan, J. D. Riley, A. E. Berry, James B. Taylor, and Agent Miller were to go through an alley in the back of the station to confront the outlaws from the rear. Meanwhile, Chief of Police H. D. Harper, Officer Thomas Shockley, and Sergeant Reuben Webb were to use their vehicle in the front to close off the bandits' escape route.

Just past three o'clock that afternoon, Chief Harper's car left the police station, only a few seconds after the other police vehicle with the five detectives had left. The plan was to approach the bandits from both sides at the same time. Congested traffic held up the police chief's car for a couple of minutes, however, and the other vehicle reached the gas station alone about ten minutes after three. While the pillars at the station gave some protection to the criminals, the officers were mostly in the open.[6]

The detectives went through the alley to the station and stopped where Jones and Dean were standing behind the Marmon, between it and the glass front of the station. Lancaster was in the back seat. The officers argued as to whether it was the car they were looking for. Riley thought it was not the right one, but Rowan insisted it was.

Before they had time to leap out of their car, Jones reached into the Marmon for a revolver and fired three shots at the officers. Detectives Berry, Taylor, and Miller took up positions in the street. Rowan and Riley stepped from the car and saw the three gangsters.[7] "Put up your hands," the officers demanded.[8] The instant Rowan left the side of the police vehicle, Jones fired one shot at the officer, who immediately returned the gunfire. Rowan then crouched low to the ground and went toward the Marmon.[9]

A rain of dozens of shots followed from both sides. Jones fired about twenty times and must have used three or four revolvers, because he did not stop to reload. The big French plate-glass windows in front of the station were pierced in scores of places, and many of the shots lodged in the ceiling, with most shots going high. Two wild shots from the excited and anxious bandits entered the nearby Moyer auction house.[10] As Rowan went up to the vehicle, Dean, who wasn't participating in the gun battle, rushed around the Marmon and yelled, "Don't shoot my husband!"[11]

Lancaster used .38-special revolvers. After emptying his first gun, he took up another one. The gangster turned around and fired two shots at Rowan only a few feet away, one of them taking effect. Hit in his right shoulder at an angle, the officer dropped. The bullet went just back of the right collar bone and took a course downward and forward, severing the pulmonary artery and the right ventricle before exiting from the stomach. Another bullet struck Rowan's watch, freezing it at 3:10 p.m. As he collapsed, Rowan fired one more shot.[12]

Kansas City Blackie turned his attention to Riley. The officer grabbed a sawed-off shotgun and jammed shells into it. He fired as he ran toward the Marmon. About eight feet from the vehicle, Riley leaped behind a brick pillar and leveled his shotgun at Blackie. Just as the officer started to pull the trigger, the elderly woman driver stepped into range, and he hesitated a minute before shooting.

His fourth shot emptied the shotgun. Riley threw it down, jerked out a revolver, and fired at Lancaster once. A shot from the gangster tore off one of Riley's fingers and knocked the officer's revolver out of his right hand. Riley started to reach for his other pistol, but was hit in his left eye, with the bullet stopping near his brain. That knocked Riley cold for a few seconds, and he thought he had been killed, but the next thing the officer remembered was being shot again through the right hand and the right foot. Flying fragments of brick from the pillar so disfigured his countenance that Riley was unrecognizable after he fell in the battle. His whole lacerated face was black and blue.

Meanwhile, the Hudson's windshield was shattered and its elderly woman driver was still at the pump frozen with fear. Henderson bravely rushed to the woman, put her into the car and drove out of harm's way.

The police chief's car with the three officers came up and stopped in front of the station. With Jones at the wheel, Dean jumped into the Marmon.

Jones rapidly drove the vehicle backward from the station. The couple were in the front seats, with Kansas City Blackie in the back. Dean was holding her side as though she had been wounded. Lancaster, his flesh torn away and with a bloody face and head, was bleeding from his right cheek.

The officers were prepared to shoot, but a passing streetcar and the crowd in the street made it almost impossible to fire for fear of injuring or killing bystanders. Nevertheless all the officers took shots at the bandits. The gangsters swept past, firing at the policemen. One shot missed an officer in the police chief's vehicle by a fraction of an inch. Two bullets hit the big Case police car.[13] Jones fired at Chief Harper standing in the street near the Moyer auction house, while Blackie fired toward the prostrate Riley.[14] The police chased the gangsters, but soon lost them, and the unarmed city fire chief followed them in his roadster until it developed engine trouble.[15]

Two mechanics from the station reached the badly wounded Rowan and placed him into an automobile. One mechanic drove him to the hospital. Still clutching his revolver with two discharged cartridges, Rowan, unable to talk, died from internal hemorrhages en route to the hospital.[16]

According to the local newspaper:

> *No man in Colorado was feared more by criminals nor trusted more fully by his friends than John W. Rowan…He died with a gun in his hand, his last voluntary movement being a final shot at the desperadoes, who had already fired a fatal bullet into his body…He is survived by his wife and son Chester.*[17]

Riley survived, but suffered permanent injuries. He had been on the plainclothes force for some time and had been a candidate for constable on the Republican ticket.

While Rowan was killed and Riley severely wounded, "everyone marveled at the fact that no member of the bandit party apparently had been injured despite the fact that half a dozen men were literally pouring buckshot, rifle and revolver bullets in the machine at close range."[18] In fact, Lancaster had been hit five times in his right leg and once on the right side of his head.[19]

A "ring of steel" of more than one hundred miles in diameter was put around the city.[20] As the *Colorado Springs Gazette* reported:

> *Five minutes after the shooting occurred, fully 200 Colorado Springs men, armed, were in search for the party. Within two hours after the shooting, every road leading from Colorado Springs was guarded, and every town within a radius of 100 miles had been notified and furnished with a description of the fleeing bandits.*
>
> *There have been murder stories, tales of crimes as dastardly and as brutal as this, of whole-sale slaughter by paid killers, but never in the history of Colorado has a murder narrative developed as quickly….and finally resolved itself into so great a mystery as has the slaying of "Johnny" Rowan and the vanishing murderers….*
>
> *The stories of their escapades, their close scrapes with the police, their terrorizing and murderous plunder, reads like an extract from the most spectacular of dime novels….The wildest night that Colorado Springs ever witnessed—a night when every man carried a gun: when there was talk of lynching and hanging: when [the] police department and civilians united in a chase and manhunt that covered [the] surrounding territory for a radius of 25 miles.*[21]

CHAPTER 22:

MORE VIOLENCE

Meanwhile in Denver, the police had located the gang's hideout at 815 East Seventeenth Avenue. Inside were Frank; his wife, baby, mother, and stepfather; Sherrill; Eudaley; and Eva. Nine police officers surrounded the hideout and waited for them to come out.

Finally at eight o'clock the night of the Colorado Springs shootout, Eva, Sherrill, and Eudaley walked from the house and jumped into a car parked nearby. When Frank came out and headed for the vehicle five minutes later, the police opened fire without warning. Sherrill, at the wheel, didn't wait for Lewis, but drove rapidly through an alley, the only escape route not guarded by the police. Sherrill, hit once in his left knee, drove the bullet-ridden car with one hand and fired over his shoulder with the other. Eva's hat flew off. Detectives Harry Lane and Herbert M. Cole were slightly wounded. Officers pursued, but soon lost them.[1]

The officers' full attention was on the escaping gangsters. Lewis was able to run back into the house and out the rear door, which had been left unguarded. A few minutes later, policemen entered the house and arrested the two Bubbs and Frank's wife. Meanwhile, the gangster took a cab and told the driver he would give him thirty dollars to take him to Colorado Springs.[2]

At the Denver city limits, a large vehicle driven by W. D. Otter of Denver approached the three fugitives' car. With Otter was Mildred Waco Gates, a young woman from Dallas. Sherrill pulled directly across the road, forcing Otter to make a sudden stop. The bandits climbed into Otter's car and drove toward Colorado Springs for several miles until they came to an isolated schoolhouse. Otter's and Gates's hands and feet were tied with wire, and they were left in the schoolyard. The bandits took money and valuables from the couple. To replace her lost hat, Eva took a pretty hat from Mildred.[3]

"Shoot 'em and get them out of the way!" Eva shouted.[4] Sherrill refused to do anything and then drove off. An hour later the couple freed themselves, found a telephone, and called the police.[5]

Meanwhile, at 10:15 p.m. the taxicab carrying Frank passed by a large posse at Palmer Lake and was stopped.[6]

"Get out of that car and stick up your arms," yelled an officer.[7]

With his hands up, the outlaw—without a hat and in his shirt sleeves—came out of the cab and was handcuffed. Very excited, Lewis said a man had just eloped with his wife, and he was trying to catch them.[8]

"That stuff don't go with us," cried a voice.[9]

After a quick search, three revolvers and a quantity of ammunition were found in the taxicab, and Lewis was taken to the Colorado Springs jail. More than $1,200 in cash was discovered in his pockets. Lewis was not positively identified until a deputy sheriff saw a tattoo of a woman on his arm.[10]

"Wait a minute, gentlemen," the gangster said at the jail. He took out an automatic pistol hidden by his trouser leg. He placed the gun on a desk. "Here you are," he said.[11] The outlaw could not pay his $25,000 bond for train robbery.[12]

Jesse James Jr., son of the notorious outlaw, was Lewis's attorney. James had been born on August 31, 1875, in Nashville, Tennessee. As a young man, he used the alias of Tim Edwards to conceal his notorious family relationships. James practiced law in Kansas City, Missouri, and Los Angeles. He wrote a book titled *Jesse James Was My Father* and appeared in two films in 1921, *Jesse James Under the Black Flag* and *Jesse James as the Outlaw*.[13]

Meanwhile Sherrill, who was driving, and his two companions drove slowly down a very dark dirt road that was in terrible condition. It came to an abrupt end, so the outlaw headed his vehicle back toward Colorado Springs.[14]

A posse of several hundred men at Sedalia, twenty miles south of Denver, saw two cars rapidly approaching at two thirty that morning. An officer stepped out into the road and commanded the drivers of the vehicles to halt. A Ford car, driven by two young men from Denver, stopped. The Hudson Super-Six, however, whirled around the officer and went south down Castle Rock Road. As they passed the posse members posted along the road in a ditch, the bandits fired out both sides of their bullet-ridden car. Dirt was thrown over the guardsmen. About seventy-five shots were fired at the trio.

The bandits' car proceeded about a hundred yards farther, swerved off the road to the right, and stopped. As Sherrill fell out of the vehicle, wounded in both legs, Eva ran around the front of the car in the glare of the headlights and raised her hands, crying that she had surrendered. Sherrill and Eudaley, unhurt, escaped into the woods. Eva, also unhurt, could not see because of the bright lights. When she got in front of the car and threw up her hands, posse members thought it might be a trap or ruse to allow Sherrill and Eudaley to escape. They did not go up to the car. She cried, "Boys, don't shoot me."[15]

The posse men threw their spotlight on her and told her to come in. Eva was carefully searched and no weapons found. She gave her age as nineteen years, but those who saw her thought she looked much older, had a hard-looking face, and was very cool and deliberate in her every motion. She would not talk.[16] They took Eva to the depot at Sedalia, searched her again, and placed her under guard.

Three automatic rifles, three six-shooters, a satchel filed with ammunition of all kinds, and four other automobile license tags, all from different states, were found in the bandits' car.

A party searched the brush alongside the road to the west. Sherrill, groaning in severe pain and lying on the ground about a hundred yards from the road with three wounds in his left knee and one in the right leg, was discovered by about ten members of the Reserve Watch, four citizens of Sedalia, and a government forest ranger.[17] Someone fired a shotgun at him. Although ordered to rise, Sherrill could not.[18] He kept asking to be taken to a hospital and yelled that it was inhuman to let him lie there and suffer. A posse member spoke up to say he had failed to think of that when members of his gang shot and killed Johnny Rowan and tried to kill several others.[19]

"Where is that kid that fired the shotgun at me? I would like to shake that bird's hand—he sure is a peach," Sherrill said.[20] The posse carried him to a nearby store, laid him down, and called a doctor from Castle Rock. About that time, the Denver police arrived and took charge of the prisoners. A couple hours later Eudaley was discovered sound asleep in the woods.[21]

Jones, Dean, and Lancaster fled to the gang hideout in Denver. At one thirty in the morning on September 14, someone shouted at them from the front yard. As Dean went to the door, Jones and Kansas City Blackie hid on both sides of the door. A man came to the door and asked, "Who are you?"

Jones confronted the man and pressed a gun in his stomach. "Hands up," ordered Jones.

Thinking Jones was a Pinkerton detective, the officer responded, "But I'm Ryan, Officer Ryan." Patrolmen John Ryan and Harry Wilson had been at the house in case any of the gangsters returned. At the other side of the house, Wilson heard voices and hurried to the front door, pulling out his gun. Lancaster shot off one of his fingers, and the officer's revolver dropped to the floor.

"Now hands up!" yelled Jones. The officers did as they were told. The lawmen's firearms were taken and they were tied up inside the house.[22]

The three criminals broke into a Denver gas station for oil and gas about three in the morning of September 14. Jones jumped out of the car, walked up to the locked door, and got inside by using a hammer. He returned to their vehicle and filled it up.

Meanwhile, the thirty-five-year-old motorcycle officer Luther McMahill rang in his last report about a half-an-hour later. McMahill, a brick mason, had joined the force in 1913 and had a good record. Ten minutes later, as he rode home on a bicycle, he saw a man and woman in a large high-powered touring car without lights in the shadow of some trees. Nearby was Lancaster. The officer went up to them, drew his flashlight, and turned it on the occupants of the vehicle. Without any preliminaries, Jones, in the driver's seat, shot the officer dead with a revolver, the bullet striking him directly above the heart.

As Jones started the car, Lancaster jumped onto the running board while it was in motion.[23] "All right. Here, get in. Let's go," Jones said.[24] Lucky again, the couple was unhurt, and Lancaster had received no further wounds. The trio headed toward Kansas City. A two thousand dollar bounty was placed on their heads.[25]

CHAPTER 23:

"THE MOST SPECTACULAR GUNFIGHT EVER WITNESSED IN THE CITY"

Jones, Dean, and Lancaster eluded thousands of police on their way to Kansas City. It remains a mystery how they did so.[1] Kansas City Blackie and Jones were suspected of again attempting to rob Katy train No. 27 near Iola, Kansas, on the night of September 16, 1918, but an unexpected freight car came ahead of the passenger car, foiling the robbery. The bandits escaped in a waiting vehicle. It is unlikely the wounded Blackie was involved.[2]

Jones and Lancaster in another Marmon car drove up in front of the two-story brick Lancaster home in Kansas City, Missouri, about one in the afternoon on Thursday, September 19. Lancaster's brother Warren carried the wounded criminal into the house and put him into bed. Warren asked what was wrong.[3] "The cops in Colorado Springs sure gave us hell," Blackie replied.[4]

Jones brought into the house a first-aid kit containing bandages and doctor's instruments. Blackie never left the house again, fearing he might be "turned up" to the police if he called a doctor. Instead he decided to treat himself with bandages and medicines.

Two days later, at one in the morning, Jones made his last visit to the house. The gangster honked his horn, and Kansas City Blackie hobbled outside and talked with him for about one hour. The Lancaster brothers would not see Jones again.[5]

Jones and another man robbed the First State Bank at Savanna, Oklahoma, seven miles south of McAlester, at three o'clock the afternoon of September 24. The masked men locked cashier A. L. Either into the vault and fled with $1,500. Either was able to get out within a few minutes and gave the alarm. The posse was in close pursuit, and a few miles from Savanna, a pitched battle between the bandits and the posse occurred. One bandit was believed to be wounded, but they managed to get away.[6] On that same day, Sherrill underwent an operation for the removal of bullets from his legs.[7]

A tip given by Jones, who had fought with Lancaster over the division of loot, led police to raid Lancaster's hideout at 1904 Montgall Avenue on September 24. Sherrill also gave information that located Kansas City Blackie. Police at the Flora Avenue Station were told at 1:45 p.m. that members of the Lewis-Jones gang had returned from Colorado and had just entered the house. Chief Godley ordered Sergeant W. H. Tobenor, drill master of the police department, to the house. Near the house, Tobenor was joined by patrolmen Al Bennett and William Wiebold and by John Porter, a soldier.

As the police car stopped in front of the house, a woman on the front porch noticed the officers and ran into the house. She refused to open the door when they knocked on the front door. The officers then went to the locked rear door.[8] "Open that door before we knock it in," screamed Sergeant Tobenor. "Beat it, Blackie, it's the cops," the woman yelled upstairs.[9]

Believing that someone might flee through the front door, the officers returned there. Warren Lancaster opened the door and was arrested. After putting him into the patrol wagon, the policemen went back and found that the woman had fled. Warren denied there were any women with Jones and his brother. Jones was falsely believed to have been in the house during the battle, although the Lancaster brothers told police the gangster was not there.

The officers started upstairs to the second floor. At the stop of the stairs, Blackie called out, "Who are you?"

"Police officers," they responded.[10]

Kansas City Blackie fired at the officers with a revolver. A bullet grazed Sergeant Tobenor's forehead, another hit Patrolman Bennett below the knee of his right leg, another struck Patrolman Wiebold, and one hit the soldier. Wounded, the officers retreated to the street in front of the house. However, the wounds were not serious.[11]

Since they were in a dangerous gunfight, the policemen called headquarters for backup. A good distance from the house, 125 officers took cover and began firing. Lancaster, well supplied with arms and ammunition, barricaded himself inside the house; using a mattress as a shield, he fired a rain of shots incessantly from second-story windows. Three revolvers and an automatic rifle with many cartridges were in the house. Thousands of rounds of ammunition were fired.[12] The gun battle "was the most spectacular ever witnessed" in the city, according to a newspaper account. A crowd estimated at five thousand people gathered nearby and watched the action. Three officers were forced out of action, but were not seriously wounded.[13]

After more than two hours, the firing from the house ceased, and it became quiet. Detectives entered the house. Blackie threw up his hands, shouting, "Come and get me. I'm alone." The fugitive, surrounded by many empty shells, was mortally wounded with a dozen wounds, two of which traversed his body.

On the way to the hospital, Blackie admitted his identity and said he had come into the city in an auto with Dale Jones and two women, who had left immediately for Indianapolis on a train. Jones's capture was soon expected.[14] At the hospital, Blackie told police he had been seriously injured at the battle at the hands of "that dick that kept shooting at me from behind that brick post," meaning J. D. Riley.

He answered a few deathbed questions asked him by an assistant prosecutor:

"What is your name?"

"I'm Kansas City Blackie," he answered.

"Where are the rest of the bunch, Blackie?"

Lancaster did not answer.

"How did you get here?"

"Drove."

"What car were you in?"

"Marmon."

"Who drove it here from Denver?"

"I did."

"Who was with you in Denver?"

"Dale Jones."

"Where's Dale now?"

"Don't know."

"Who's the leader of the gang, Blackie?"

"Dale Jones."

"Well, where is he now?"

"I don't know."

"When did he leave?"

"Night before last."

Lancaster died about an hour later.[15]

On September 27, Frank Knight was arrested in Kansas City, Missouri, and accused of train robbery. Lewis and Sherrill faced the same charge.[16] Four days later, police fished the gangsters' Marmon sedan, ridden with more than forty bullet holes, out of the Missouri River.[17]

Frank Lewis would end up serving no prison time. On October 16, 1918, at 4:30 p.m., he died at the Topeka, Kansas, jail, supposedly from the influenza epidemic. He was found dead in his cell by a guard; he had been dead for more than an hour.[18] An autopsy revealed his chest was filled with bullets, negating the theory that Spanish influenza had killed him. A bullet in the heart cavity, with a growth around it, had stopped his heart activity, and Lewis had died instantly. Although the autopsy results seemed impossible, postal inspectors insisted it was absolutely true. It was amazing that any one of the bullets had not killed him earlier.[19]

CHAPTER 24:

"YOUR LIFE IS IN GREAT DANGER"

A massive manhunt was on for Jones and Dean. They had been overheard at a gas station saying they wanted to get into the movies, so the search was centered in Los Angeles. It was thought they may have fled the country entirely. An important clue was a rare perfume on a woman's handkerchief, apparently owned by Dean, found in one of their hideouts. The Pinkertons found a Los Angeles store that sold the perfume. A woman who had purchased the perfume in the middle of November matched the description of Dean. She had given the name of Mrs. Charles Forbes and said she lived in a bungalow on Sierra Madre Avenue.[1]

The couple were suspects in the murder of Reuben Fogel, a wealthy real-estate operator who was lured to a vacant house in Los Angeles on October 29, 1918, and beaten to death. A woman took part in that crime, and her traces, such as brass hairpins, were found in the house.

Two weeks before the murder, Fogel and a man he worked with had visited a woman spiritualist medium. She told the real-estate operator that the back screen door of a house would be cut, he would lose some money, and his life was in great danger. Fogel hurried to his Santa Monica home thinking burglars might have entered his house.

At two thirty the afternoon of October 29, Fogel received a telephone call from a woman who said she was an aged and invalid woman who had a $500 Liberty bond she would sell for $490. Fogel, who often bought bonds, secured $490 from a bank and went to the address given to him. He asked three boys to direct him to the house of "Mrs. Robinson no. 429 west 27th street." The boys did not know of anyone with that name nearby, but answered that the address was a few houses up the street. This was the last time the aged man was seen, except by his killers.

The murderers had entered the vacant rental house, a large, furnished twelve-room structure, by cutting the rear screen door. When Fogel called at three thirty that afternoon, they admitted him by the front door, led him upstairs to the library, and seated him in a chair. The male murderer then went behind him and struck him on the head seven times with something like an iron crowbar, causing six deep fractures of the skull. The first blow caused instant death. At that blow, the broker's brains were literally knocked out and spattered over the curtains and blinds of three windows. After searching him and finding an envelope containing the $490, the murderers fled out the back door about four o'clock. Three and a half hours later, a patrolman found the back door of the house open and the screen cut. He entered, searched the house, and found Fogel's body. Fogel left behind a widow, two sons, and a daughter.[2]

The Fogel murder was similar to the case of Joseph Morino, the wealthy importer of jewelry, in which Morino was lured to an apartment room in Kansas City, Missouri, by Dean and clubbed to death by Jones or Sam Taylor on May 24, 1918.[3] The police could not determine how the killers were able to flee from the house with blood-spattered hands and clothing, taking a bloody bludgeon with them, and make their getaway without being seen or even suspected.[4]

CHAPTER 25:

"TWO BRIEF AND COLORFUL LIVES"

A woman gas station attendant in Arcadia, California, a quiet little suburb of Los Angeles, called the local sheriff to report that a young man and woman who had several times purchased gas and oil at her station fit the description of the fugitives. Their pictures were often in the newspapers and widely distributed by police. Post office inspectors had told local authorities that Jones and his companion had traveled to California in a high-powered car and that Jones was missing a finger on his right hand. Deputy sheriffs George Van Vliet and William Anderson and two Pinkerton detectives were sent to the station on Saturday, November 16, 1918.[2]

Forty-five-year-old Van Vliet, one of the most efficient deputies in the sheriff's office, had a wife and three children. He had entered the sheriff's office about fifteen years before and was involved mostly on transportation cases. Two years before, a prisoner he was bringing in from El Paso had jumped off the train. Van Vliet leaped from his Pullman berth, flung himself out a car window, and, barefooted, pursued the prisoner two miles and successfully recaptured him.[3]

The lawmen lay in wait for the bandits at the station morning and night; for three days the couple did not come. Their long vigil was rewarded at 6:20 p.m. on Tuesday, November 19. The two Pinkerton agents were not with the two deputy sheriffs.

Jones jumped out of a stolen Cadillac roadster near the station and reconnoitered while his wife remained at the wheel with the motor running, ready to dash away in case it looked suspicious. He had two automatic revolvers, while Dean had a rifle and an automatic revolver. After making a careful survey of the station, Jones leaped back into the vehicle and motioned to his wife to back the car alongside the filling pump. The couple went to the station office and bought gasoline and chocolate candy. As they returned to their car, Jones started to fill the gas tank, and Dean got into the driver's seat; the attendant then signaled the lawmen.

The deputies came out of their hiding places behind a shed in the back with sawed-off shotguns. They crept around each side of the station. Van Vliet went to the back of the car while Anderson headed for the front.[4] "Throw up your hands," they demanded.

"You've got me!" Jones shouted.[5] The gangster faced the officers behind the car and pretended to throw up his hands, but as he brought up his right hand he drew an automatic revolver from a holster under his left arm and fired point-blank at Van Vliet. A bullet went through Van Vliet's body, not two inches from his heart; the lawman fell mortally wounded without firing a shot.

During the next sixty seconds, twenty shots were fired. A soldier, Private Alfred Brook from the nearby Army Balloon School, who was waiting for a ride into Los Angeles, was hit in his back by a stray bullet and fell to the grass unconscious. Dean whipped out an automatic revolver from a car door pocket and fired at Anderson, empting the gun with three quick shots. She then picked up a rifle from the rear of the vehicle, put it on a swivel in the car and fired twice, one bullet passing through the left sleeve of Anderson's coat, a few inches from his heart, and the second passing through the coat, grazing the skin also near the heart.

The deputy sheriff fired twice at the woman with his sawed-off shotgun. Half a dozen buckshot entered the right side of her head, other buckshot hit her right leg, and she tumbled over dead. The automobile engine was still running.

Anderson then fired at Jones; the shot seemed to wound the desperado, for Jones dropped to one knee. Meanwhile, the gangster, half-concealed behind the car hood, fired several shots. Anderson had only one shell left, and it was kill or be killed. The lawman dodged behind the station and dropped to the ground. He stood when Jones slowly raised himself to look over the hood. Jumping out, Anderson fired his last shot, hitting the gangster in the back of his head, tearing away part of his skull. As he fell, Jones kept firing from a second automatic he had pulled from a belt. There was not a full cartridge in his gun when he lost consciousness. With one shot, Anderson had killed the bandit.

At that moment, the gang that had spread terror throughout the West for the past six years was totally annihilated. Van Vliet was taken to the Army Balloon School Hospital. At first it was thought he had an even chance of surviving, but four hours later, he died. Jones died while being taken to the same hospital. Private Brook completely recovered.

A search of the bandits' home found two more Winchester rifles, a sawed-off repeating shotgun, two heavy-caliber automatic revolvers, a black handbag full of ammunition, and dies for changing the numbers on automotive engines. Some $208,000 was later recovered from the accounts of Eva Lewis.[6]

The gangster couple were saved from burial in the Potter's field by Dean's mother. She provided a common grave for the pair in Calvary Cemetery, near Monrovia, California, where they were buried on November 25, 1918. Present at the funeral were Mrs. Celano and Mr. and Mrs. Ray Nieinever. Dean (given name Marie Celano) was a sister of Mrs. Nieinever.[7]

Like Bonnie and Clyde some years later, the couple died in a car ambush. As one writer put it, "Two brief and colorful lives, buried at Carmel-by-the-Sea, just as they died, side by side."[8]

CHAPTER 26:

THE FALL OF MATTIE HOWARD

Mattie Howard and Sam Taylor had been arrested at Howard's mother's home in Raton, New Mexico, on June 22, 1918, after the murder of Joseph Morino that May, and were taken to Kansas City, Missouri. For some inexplicable reason, the courts were generous to Mattie. Her bond was set at $10,000, later reduced to $5,000. Jesse James Jr. was her lawyer.

Howard joined the Tony Cruye gang, which specialized in car thefts and highway robbery.[1] The thirty-eight-year-old Cruye had been born and raised in Kansas City, Missouri. His gang attempted to rob a poker game at the Merchants Hotel in Kansas City, Missouri, on August 25, 1919.

Fred West, clerk of the Merchants Hotel, was in the hotel lobby shortly after four o'clock in the morning when Tony Cruye and his three companions entered and asked to be shown room 401, occupied by fifty-four-year-old Fred Young.

Young, who was winning the game, had gone back to playing poker about a half hour before the four gangsters appeared. The game had begun the previous afternoon in room 403, connected to room 401, and continued into the morning.

The gangsters and West rode in the elevator to the fourth floor. As they stepped into the hallway, they drew revolvers, cursed West, told him to shut his mouth, and then pulled masks from their pockets. The clerk led them to room 401.

No light was showing over the transom. There was a light in 403, however, and they heard subdued voices. Cruye tried the door knob, but it was locked. West rapped on the door. When there was no response, Cruye shoved West aside and began kicking in the door. Finally he tore off the lock, and the door fell open.

The four gamblers had heard the rap at the door. As they were too busy playing in room 403, they did not open the door. The door being kicked in caused them to think bandits were in the hallway. As Young ran into room 401 to get his revolver, he saw the door open and masked men with drawn revolvers trying to get inside at the same time.

As Cruye yelled, "Hands up," Young, a revolver in his right hand, fired at him, After Cruye was struck in the right lung, he staggered toward the elevator, entered it, pushed the button for the first floor, and died by the time the elevator stopped. The other three gangsters ran down the stairs and out the front door before West could shoot.

The gambler hurried into room 403 and knocked out a window screen opening onto a fire escape. The clerk yelled for help as he hurried down. He saw the three gangsters running past the hotel and Patrolman Paul Willig nearby. "Stop the running men," he yelled to the patrolman. Willig took out after them, shouting for them to halt. He fired at them when they refused to do so, hitting one of the bandits in the right thigh.

The other two criminals were arrested by another patrolman who had heard the shooting. The wounded gangster was taken to General Hospital. Young was taken to police headquarters, where they found $826 in his pockets. Young did not know the gangsters or how they learned about the poker game at the Merchants Hotel. He said, "It serves this Cruye fellow right for butting in on a friendly game." A patrolman suggested Young be given a medal for killing Cruye.[2]

In October 1919, police raided a house in St. Louis and found Howard, Taylor, and George and Marie Pappas, a sister of Howard. They discovered a jar of nitroglycerin, burglary tools, many keys, a box of percussion caps and fuses, and loaded guns. All four were arrested. On Howard they found a map on which blue ink marked the location of banks and gas stations. Red ink marked other locations, which police found were of safes that had been looted. Howard and Taylor were taken to Kansas City.[3]

Immediately, on October 20, Howard was put on trial. A taxicab driver testified he had picked up two women and a man at the Touraine Apartment Hotel early on the morning after the murder of Joseph Morino in May and recognized Taylor and Howard. He did not know the identity of the other "woman" (i.e., Dale Jones). Howard was convicted of second-degree murder on October 25 and again released on a bond of $12,000, pending appeal.[5]

On the first day of Howard's trial, three gangsters, including Mattie's lover, Albert Pagle, who had been released from prison and had robbed post offices in the Kansas City region, broke into a bookmaker's office. Someone noticed through a window two of the burglars working on a safe and told a policeman what he had seen. Officers rushed to the scene. In the following gun battle, one of the burglars was killed. An officer was shot down. As he lay on the sidewalk, Pagle shot the officer again. The two surviving gangsters escaped. A taxi driver identified Pagle as the killer. Questioned by police, Howard told them she had broken off their relationship months before.[5]

On March 9, 1920, the South Side Bank in Kansas City, Missouri, was robbed by three men just before opening time at nine in the morning. One bandit was at the wheel of a car. Inside the bank was cashier Glen

Shockey, a woman bookkeeper, and a janitor. The bandits drew revolvers and asked for the bank's money. Shockey grabbed a .41-caliber Belgian gun from a cash drawer. Shots were exchanged, and the cashier fell dead. Two assailants were wounded. The gangsters fled without getting any money. A trail of blood led from the bank to the robbers' vehicle at the curb.

The next day a newspaper reporter gave a tip as to the location of the robbers. The police raided a house owned by the notorious brothers George and James Evans, well-known fences. One of the brothers was later killed by police. Pagle lay on a bed in the Evans house, dying from a bullet wound. At the hospital where he was taken, he said his name was James Morgan. Surgeons found a .41-caliber bullet of Belgian manufacture.

Mattie Howard went to the hospital at midnight to see her lover. "Albert!" she screamed and then collapsed. Pagle died a few hours later. Mattie again collapsed at the funeral home where Pagle's body was sent.[6]

Later, on May 19, 1920, Taylor stood trial for the Morino murder and was sentenced to life imprisonment for first-degree murder.[7]

On May 25, 1921, Howard's sentence was affirmed by the Missouri Supreme Court. She could not be found, and her bond was forfeited. A $500 reward was offered for her capture by her bondsman, Jesse James Jr. On November 15, Howard was arrested at a Memphis, Tennessee, pawn shop and returned to Kansas City, Missouri. Three days later she was incarcerated in the Missouri State Penitentiary.[8]

EPILOGUE

After her release from prison on May 17, 1928,[1] Mattie "Agate Eyes" Howard was heard of again in Colorado, where she became an evangelist and wrote a book.[2] As late as 1970, an article about Howard appeared in the *Los Angeles Times,* but did not make any reference to her criminal past.[3]

Roy Joe Lewis had been convicted of first-degree murder in December 1916 and sentenced to his natural life from January 10, 1917. Lewis, a model prisoner, was received during January 1917 and paroled on January 7, 1941.[4] For years Lewis had been a trusty, allowed to leave the penitentiary while serving as chauffeur for several wardens of the prison. Four wardens recommended his parole.

Missouri Governor Lloyd C. Stark granted the parole based on Lewis's having been a model prisoner and evidence showing he was not the one who fired the fatal shot. He was paroled to a Kansas City man who obtained a job for him at a Denver packing plant. The St. Louis Police Department opposed the parole.[5]

Lewis later moved to Springfield, Missouri, where he worked as a service-station operator. He was active in the Baptist Church. Roy married and had a daughter, a son, two stepsons, and nine grandchildren. He died on August 4, 1972.[6]

In contrast to Roy, his brother Ora had a terrible record. In December 1916 he had been convicted of first-degree murder. Ora was given a death sentence, which was later changed to life imprisonment. He was received at the prison during January 1917.[7]

At eight o'clock on the night of June 12, 1920, Ora, Johjn Shead, and William Stender of St. Louis, who had served three years and three months of a ten-year sentence for robbery, were in adjoining cells. Somehow, Stender had obtained keys for the cell doors. The three men opened the doors simultaneously and leaped on a guard who was passing in the corridor.

Running outside the prison building, the three still had to get outside the wall. They jumped into an empty coal car that sat at the top of a steep grade and released the brake. The steel car went down the grade, a distance of fifty yards, and crashed through the twelve-foot-high steel gate. The car was not derailed and ran on outside the gate toward the Missouri Pacific Railroad tracks. As it stopped on an upgrade, the prisoners jumped out. Lewis and Shead were soon caught by the night yardmaster and his assistant. They offered no resistance. Prison guards and local police searched for Stender, but could not find him.[8]

Ora escaped once again from the Marion Sawmill, fifteen miles west of the prison, on Sunday night, April 23, 1939, with Ted Larue, who had been sentenced to fifteen years for robbery, and Christ Herdbru, serving five years for robbery. The next day a city detective, Jack Clifford Sr., who had arrested Lewis in 1916, was given the job of finding the escaped prisoners. A tip led to the arrests of Herdbru and Larue without resistance as they left an empty building that night in Jefferson City. Lewis, believed to be heavily armed, eluded the officers by slipping out of the building before their arrival.

Lewis was picked up the next day and driven to St. Louis by Joseph Chouteau, a former convict, and his wife. His friend later was arrested and served two years for aiding his escape.[9] The gangster was returned from New Orleans on October 30. He had been arrested there on the night of October 24 on a charge of breaking into a saloon and taking $11.70.

Lewis said rigors of the lumber camp forced him to escape, adding he "preferred death to staying in that camp." Actually, Lewis had been sent to the camp "for his health at his own request," according to prison officials. Penal Director Grover C. Clevenger said, "I understand he was sent there at his own request. As for Lewis's assertion that the work was too hard—that's a joke." Other prison officials thought that the criminal "looked bad" after being at the prison for twenty years. The late warden Frank Ramsey believed the fresh air at the lumber camp "would do him good." "All the prisoners want to go to the lumber camp," Clevenger continued. "They're well-fed there and there is no close supervision. The work isn't hard."[10]

Ora Lewis was discharged on March 18, 1947, but his parole was revoked on August 15, 1949. Next, he was discharged on June 15, 1951. He was returned on July 30, 1953. Finally, the convict was permanently discharged on March 7, 1958.[11] Lewis died on July 9, 1958, at Joplin, Missouri, after a long illness.[12]

Roy Sherrill was sentenced on November 11, 1918, to twenty-five years for mail robbery and was received at Leavenworth two days later.[13] On that date Sherrill said:

> *If I had not got shot in the fight at Denver I would have deserted the gang anyhow. I was tired of the gang and tired of getting the worst of it. The only thing that hurts me is the fact that I have disgraced my sisters, brothers and parents. I intend to serve my time and make the best record I can. I am done with it all and I am done with crime.*[14]

His sentence was commuted to ten years by order of President Wilson on April 21, 1920.[15] Later, on June 22, 1921, he escaped in a prison doctor's car with a convict named Joe Davis. Davis was later recaptured at Topeka, Kansas.[16] Over the next two years, Sherrill was suspected in several highway robberies, as well as one near the Denver mint.

On December 18, 1922, five bandits robbed a Federal Reserve Bank truck of $200,000 and killed guard Charles Linton near the United States Mint at Denver. A wounded gang member was carried away by his partners. Following his arrest in 1918, Sherrill had told authorities that the Lewis-Jones gang had made detailed plans for the robbery of the mint, but his confession was believed to be "too fanciful to be believable."[17]

On May 24, 1923, three men were arrested near Scipio in Pittsburg County, Oklahoma, when their high-powered car became marooned by water. The police found two rifles, four six-shooters, five hundred rounds of ammo, a gallon of whiskey, and safe-blowing gear. The trio gave their names as Homer Johnson, Bart Clark, and Jack Lacey. They were put in the McAlester, Oklahoma, jail, and fingerprint checks revealed that Lacey, alias James Murphy, alias Jack Conway, and alias Jack Arlington, had served time in Leavenworth for robbery at Fort Bliss, Texas, and had also been arrested at Elko, Nevada, and San Bernardino, California. Clark, alias Les Cruce, was a notorious Kansas City bandit believed to have been killed some months before. Johnson was, in fact, Roy Sherrill, out of prison for 710 days, with at least ten known aliases.

During Sherrill's escape, they had engaged in a number of highway robberies.[18] Around June 3, 1923, Sherrill was sent back to Leavenworth to complete his ten-year prison term, with the loss of all good time. He was transferred to the Atlanta Penitentiary on July 25, 1926, and was released from Atlanta on February 7, 1930. He was discharged from supervision on January 7, 1931.[19] During World War Two, he worked at a defense plant in Indiana.[20]

On January 21, 1919, a man posing as a jeweler named J. H. Smith, tried to dispose of some valuable jewelry at an assay office in Portland, Oregon. The manager called the police, and Smith was confronted by Detective J. M. Tackaberry, who shot him dead when he resisted. Smith was believed to be E. O. Lancaster of Minneapolis, a brother of the notorious Roscoe Lancaster. However, Roscoe had no brother named E. O.

On June 24, 1926, thirty-five-year-old Harry H. Lancaster, another brother of Roscoe, was arrested in Kansas City when detectives caught him coming out of a store with a bundle of clothes. Taken to the local jail, he committed suicide later that day by hanging himself with his own belt. He had escaped from the Columbus, Kansas, jail on May 12 while awaiting trial for boxcar robbery, and he had served three prison terms in Missouri and one in Kansas.

On November 13, 1929, when an old house in Kansas City, Kansas, was being torn down, workers found a skeleton of a person who had apparently been killed by a blow to the head, but authorities were unable to say whether it was a man or woman. Local inhabitants said that years before, the house had been briefly occupied by "the notorious Dale Jones gang" and the theory was advanced that the body was that of a slain gang member.[21]

In May 1914, John Shead was sentenced to life in prison, beginning June 20, 1914. He was received at the Missouri state prison on June 22, 1914, and discharged on February 8, 1952.[22]

George Eudaley (alias Ray Long) was sentenced in January 1919 to twenty-five to thirty years for robbery with a dangerous weapon. The convict was received at the Colorado State Penitentiary on January 9, 1919, and was paroled on May 24, 1930.[23]

Thomas King (whose aliases included Thomas Knight and Earl King) was sentenced on November 11, 1918, to twenty-five years and was received at Leavenworth on November 13, 1918. Parole was denied on January 17, 1927. King, who feared that other convicts would kill him, was transferred to St. Elizabeth Mental Hospital on March 20, 1928.[24]

On January 14, 1919, Eva Lewis was sentenced to five to seven years for robbery with a dangerous weapon, and was received at the Colorado prison later that month. Her occupation was listed as "chorus girl." She was paroled on November 30, 1922, and discharged in December 1922,[25] about ten days before the famous Denver mint robbery in which Roy Sherrill was suspected. By that time she was a paralytic. After the robbery, she was arrested and grilled intensively. Denying any part in the robbery, she said, "It was too deliberately conceived for a woman to take part in it." A few days later, she collapsed on her mother's floor and apparently lost the power of speech, due to what her doctors called a "hysterical stupor." She was a victim of aphasia and lay pale and emaciated, but still beautiful.[26]

The Pinkertons at St. Louis reported on July 8, 1924, that Eva had married a man named Case, then left him and took up with a convict named Katz. Katz and Eva were living with her mother and stepfather in Kansas City, Missouri. The Pinkertons warned local police to watch her because she was still dangerous. Eventually she faded into obscurity.[27]

Also fading into obscurity were John and Martha Bubb, Oscar Lee Lewis, and Stella Landon. John Bubb died on May 23, 1952, at Kansas City, Missouri.[28]

The period from 1866 to 1936 was the golden age of crime when criminals could become celebrities. But there is a gap of popular interest in criminals in the 1910s, between the horseback outlaws and the automobile bandits of the 1920s and 1930s.[29] In probably the last horseback bank robbery, a masked outlaw on horseback robbed the First National Bank at Hatch, New Mexico, for $2,000, on June 1, 1932.[30]

The Lewis-Jones gang deserves inclusion among the infamous criminals of the goldern age.. They may have killed up to nine police officers, as well as five citizens, maiming several more, and they stole hundreds of thousands of dollars. The following is a list of their victims:

1. The possible murder of police officer William Koger on November 22, 1913..
2. The murder of Constable Samuel Queen on November 24, 1913.
3. The murder of police officer Frank Griswold on May 20, 1915.
4. The murder of grocer William Sutton on October 9, 1915.
5. The murder of police officer John F. McKenna on April 7, 1916.
6. The murder of police officer William A. Dillon on April 7, 1916.
7. The possible murder of police officer Fred Carr on July 10, 1916.
8. The murder of an unknown man in August 1917.
9. The murder of businessman Joseph Morino on May 24, 1918.
10. The murder of police officer John Rowan on September 13, 1918.
11. The murder of police officer Luther McMahill on September 14, 1918.
12. The possible murder of businessman Reuben Fogel on October 29, 1918.
13. The murder of deputy sheriff George Van Vliet on November 19, 1918.
14. The possible murder of cab driver Sam Brown at an unknown date.

According to one account, "in the lurid crime annals of the Southwest, the crimson records of the Lewis Boys easily over matched all the rest."[31]

BIBLIOGRAPHY

BOOKS

Fifer, Barbara, and Martin Kidston. *Wanted! Wanted Posters of the Old West.* Helena, MT: Farcountry Press, 2003.

Howard, Mattie. *The Pathway of Mattie Howard (to and from Prison)*, rev. ed. New York: Pageant Press, 1963.

Johnston, Lester Douglas. *The Devil's Back Porch.* Lawrence, KS: University Press of Kansas, 1970.

Morton, James. *The Mammoth Book of Gangs.* Philadelphia, Pa., Running Press, 2012.

Nash, Jay Robert. *Encyclopedia of World Crime*. Wilmette, IL: Crime Books, Inc., 1990.

Nash, Jay Robert. *Look for the Woman: A Narrative Encyclopedia of Female Poisoners, Kidnappers, Thieves, Extortionists, Terrorists, Swindlers and Spies From Elizabethan Times to the Present.* New York: M. Evans and Company, Inc., 1981.

The True Story of the Last Crime and Capture of the "Lewis Gang." Baltimore: United States Fidelity and Guaranty Company, n.d.

ARTICLES

Bailie, R. H. "Blotting Out the Lewis Boys Gang." *Real Detective,* August 1935.

Hynd, Alan. "The Pinkertons and the Murdering Masquerader." *True Detective Mysteries,* July 1941.

King, Jeffery. "Deadly Motor Bandits: The Lewis-Jones Gang." *Western Outlaw-Lawmen Association Journal* 16, no. 1 (spring 2007): 3–14.

Watson, I. B., "The Crimson Trail: Inside the Story of the Murderous Killer Dale Jones—Kansas City's Boy Bandit," *True Detective Mysteries,* November, December 1928.

NEWSPAPERS

Colorado Springs (CO) Evening Telegraph

Colorado Springs (CO) Gazette

Denver Post

Denver Rocky Mountain News

Kansas City Star

Los Angeles Times

St. Louis Daily Globe-Democrat

St. Louis Post-Dispatch

Wichita Beacon

Wichita Eagle

PRIMARY SOURCES

US Census Bureau records.

Pinkerton Detective Agency Records. Sherrill-Lewis-Jones Gang File. Library of Congress, Manuscript Division.

Prison records.

Wanted posters.

NOTES

INTRODUCTION

1. R. H. Bailie, "Blotting Out the Lewis Boys Gang," *Real Detective*, August 1935.
2. Ibid..
3. David Murray, "The Lewis-Jones Gang" (unpublished manuscript), January 1, 2011.
4. *Parsons (Kansas) Daily Republican*, October 31, 1919.
5. *Chicago Tribune*, December 21, 1933.
6. R. D. Morgan, **Taming the Sooner State: The War Between Lawmen and Outlaws in Oklahoma and Indian Territory, 1973-1941.** Stillwater, Ok., New Forums, 2007, passim: **The Encyclopedia of American Crime**, New York, Smithmark Publishers, 1992, passim.
7. Fred Gregory, ed., *Motor Trend Presents 100 Years of the Automobile* (Los Angeles: Motor Trend, 1983), 14–15.
8. *New York Times Index* (New York: New York Times Co.), 1905.
9. Clay McShane, *The Automobile: A Chronology of Its Antecedents, Development, and Impact* (New York: Routledge, 1997), 19.

10. David Murray, "From Doane to Dillinger: Armed Robbery in America from the War of Independence to the End of the Great Depression" (unpublished manuscript). January 1, 2011.
11. Jay Robert Nash, *Encyclopedia of World Crime* (Wilmette, IL: Crime Books, Inc., 1990), 3458.
12. Morgan, **Taming the Sooner State,** passim.
13. *Los Angeles Times,* December 27, 1916.
14. Gregory, *Motor Trend Presents*, 16.
15. McShane, *The Automobile*, 19.
16. Sifakis, *American Crime*, 569–70.
17. US Federal Bureau of Investigation, *The FBI: A Centennial History, 1908–2008*, (Washington, D C: US Government Printing Office, 2008), 1–11.
18. United States Postal Inspection Service website, https://postalinspectors.uspis.gov/.

CHAPTER 1: A FAMILY OF OUTLAWS

1. Census Bureau, *1900 Census*; *1910 Census.*
2. *St. Louis Post-Dispatch,* April 14. 1916.
3. Ibid., April 13, 1916.
4. US Census Bureau, *1900 Census*; *St. Louis Globe-Democrat,* November 25, 1916; Denver police report of Eva Lewis.
5. Post Office Wanted Poster, Kansas City, MO, August 22, 1918.
6. Wanted Poster, St. Louis, MO, April 17, 1916.
7. Missouri State Prison Record of Roy Joe Lewis.
8. Denver police department identification card of Eva Lewis, 1918.
9. *St. Louis Post-Dispatch,* April 14, 1916.
10. "Galena: A Lead Mining Maven," *Legends of America* website, http://www.legendsofamerica.com/ks-galena.html.
11. *St. Louis Post-Dispatch,* April 14, 1916.
12. "Junction City," Geary County (Kansas) Historical Society & Museum, http://www.gchsweb.org/history.htm#junction)_city.

13. *Denver Post*, September 15, 1918. It is unknown if any action was ever taken against Elsworth Lewis, who continued to be a policeman in Junction City in the 1910s. See city directories of Junction City, Kansas.
14. *St. Louis Post-Dispatch*, April 14, 1916.
15. Ibid., September 24, 1916.
16. Ibid.
17. Ibid.
18. Ibid., April 15, 1916.
19. Ponca City, Oklahoma, website, http://www.poncacity.com/poncacity.htm.
20. "Cherokee," in *Columbia Encyclopedia,* 5th ed. (New York: Columbia University Press, 1993), 523.

CHAPTER 2: "BELIEVE ME WE DID SOME STEALING"

1. Bailie, "Lewis Boys Gang."
2. Post Office Wanted Poster, August 22, 1918.
3. *St. Louis Post-Dispatch,* April 15, 1916.
4. Bailie, "Lewis Boys Gang."
5. *Denver Post,* September 15, 1918.
6. Ibid., September 17, 1918.
7. Ibid., September 15, 1918.
8. *St. Louis Post-Dispatch,* April 12, 1916.
9. Ibid., April 14, 1916.
10. "Online Exhibits—Sinners and Saints, Part 3," Kansas City Historical Society website, http://www.kshs.org/p/online-exhibits-sinners-and-saints-part-3/10721.
11. "Prohibition," *Encyclopedia of Oklahoma History and Culture*, http://digital.library.okstate.edu/encyclopedia/entries/P/PR018.html.

CHAPTER 3: MURDER IN A SHOE STORE

1. I. B. Watson, "The Crimson Trail: Inside the Story of the Murderous Killer Dale Jones—Kansas City's Boy Bandit," *True Detective Mysteries,* December 1928; *Wichita Beacon,* May 24, 1915; *Wichita Eagle,* May 23, 1915.
2. *Wichita Beacon,* May 24, 1915.
3. Ibid.
4. Ibid.
5. Ibid.
6. *Wichita Eagle,* May 23, 1915.
7. Ibid.
8. Ibid., May 25, 1915.
9. Ibid.
10. Ibid., May 23, 1915.
11. Ibid., May 25, 1915.
12. "$3,450 Reward Circular for Ora Lewis, Frank Lewis, Oscar Lee Lewis," County Sheriff's Office, Wichita, KS, September 18, 1916.

CHAPTER 4: "HE'S HARD OF HEARING, DON'T SHOOT"

1. Bailie, "Lewis Boys Gang"; *St. Louis Post-Dispatch,* April 14, 1916.
2. *St. Louis Post-Dispatch,* April 15, 1916.
3. Ibid., April 14, 1916.
4. *Wichita Beacon,* October 11, 1915.
5. Ibid.
6. Ibid.
7. Ibid.
8. Ibid.
9. Ibid.
10. Ibid.

11. *Topeka Daily Capital,* April 12, 1916; *St. Louis Post-Dispatch,* April 12, 1916.
12. *St. Louis Post-Dispatch,* April 14, 1916.
13. Ibid., April 11, 1916.
14. Ibid., April 12, 1916.
15. Ibid.
16. Ibid., April 14, 1916.
17. Ibid., April 12, 1916.

CHAPTER 5: "DON'T DO THAT, DON'T DO THAT"

1. *St. Louis Post-Dispatch,* April 7, 1916.
2. *St. Louis Globe Democrat,* November 25, 1916.
3. Ibid.
4. Ibid.
5. Ibid.
6. *St. Louis Post-Dispatch,* April 12, 1916.
7. *St. Louis Globe Democrat,* November 25, 1916.
8. *St. Louis Post-Dispatch,* April 7, 12, 1916.
9. *St. Louis Globe Democrat,* November 25, 1916.
10. *St. Louis Post-Dispatch,* April 7, 12, 1916.
11. Ibid., April 12, 1916.
12. Ibid.
13. Ibid., April 14, 1916.
14. Ibid.
15. Ibid.
16. Ibid., April 12, 1916.
17. Ibid., April 14, 1916.
18. Ibid.
19. Ibid.
20. Ibid., April 8, 1916.
21. Ibid.
22. Ibid.
23. Ibid.

24. Ibid., April 9, 1916.
25. *St. Louis Globe-Democrat,* November 25, 1916.
26. *St. Louis Post-Dispatch,* April 9, 1916.
27. *St. Louis Globe Democrat,* November 25, 1916.
28. *St. Louis Post-Dispatch,* April 9, 1916.
29. Ibid., April 12, 1916.
30. *St. Louis Globe Democrat,* November 25, 1916.
31. *St. Louis Post-Dispatch,* April 12, 1916.
32. Ibid., April 8, 1916.
33. Bailie, "Lewis Boys Gang."
34. *St. Louis Post-Dispatch*, April 14, 1916.
35. Ibid., April 8, 1916.
36. Ibid., April 14, 1916.
37. Ibid., April 10, 1916.
38. Ibid., April 9, 1916.
39. Bailie, "Lewis Boys Gang."
40. *St. Louis Post-Dispatch,* April 15, 1916.
41. Walter Fontane, "The Rise and Fall of 'Dinty' Colbeck: The John Gotti of St. Louis," *Rick Porrello's America Mafia.com* website, September 2001, http://americanmafia.com/Feature_Articles_159.html.

CHAPTER 6: THE CONFESSION

1. *St. Louis Post-Dispatch,* April 12, 1916.
2. Ibid.
3. Ibid.
4. Ibid., April 11, 1916.
5. Ibid., April 12, 1916.
6. Ibid.
7. Ibid.
8. Ibid
9. Ibid.
10. Ibid.
11. "Pancho Villa," in *The Columbia Encyclopedia,* 5th ed. (New York: Columbia University Press, 1993), 2888.

CHAPTER 7: THE INQUEST

1. *St. Louis Post-Dispatch,* April 12, 1916.
2. Ibid., April 13, 1916.
3. Ibid., April 14, 1916.
4. Ibid., April 13, 1916.
5. Ibid., April 14, 1916.
6. Ibid.
7. *St. Louis Globe-Democrat,* November 25, 1916.
8. *St. Louis Post-Dispatch,* April 14, 1916.
9. Ibid.
10. Ibid.
11. Ibid., April 15, 1916. The Locomobile, called the "best built car in America," was one of the most expensive and elegant automobiles manufactured in the United States. The car company went out of business in 1929. (See the Locomobile Society of America website, http://www.locomobilesociety.com/.)
12. *St. Louis Post-Dispatch,* April 15, 1916.
13. Ibid., April 16, 1916.

CHAPTER 8: "WE BOTH DECIDED WE BETTER BLOW TOWN"

1. *Kansas City Star.* September 24, 1916. According to one report, the bandits fled to Durand, Oklahoma, where they stole an auto and headed for Detroit. After being recognized in that city by citizens who had known them in St. Louis, the bandits left Detroit on the night of August 12, 1916. They talked of going to Buenos Aires or British South Africa. The Lewis boys told police this was false. See "$3,450.00 Reward Circular for Ora Lewis, Frank, Lewis, Oscar Lee Lewis," Sheriff's Office, Wichita, Kansas, September 18, 1916.
2. *Kansas City Star,* September 24, 1916.
3. *St. Louis Globe-Democrat,* November 25, 1916.

4. *Kansas City Star,* September 24, 1916.
5. *St. Louis Globe-Democrat,* November 25, 1916.
6. *Kansas City Star,* September 24, 1916.
7. *St. Louis Globe-Democrat,* November 25, 1916.
8. Ibid., November 26, 1916.
9. Ibid., November 25, 1916.
10. *Wichita Beacon,* April 20, 1916; *Wichita Eagle,* April 21, 1916.
11. K*ansas City Star,* September 24, 1916.
12. *St. Louis Globe-Democrat,* November 25, 1916.
13. *Kansas City Star,* September 24, 1916.
14. *St. Louis Globe-Democrat,* November 25, 1916.
15. *Kansas City Star,* September 24, 1916.
16. *St. Louis Globe-Democrat,* November 25, 1916.
17. *Kansas City Journal,* July 10, 1916.
18. *St. Louis Globe-Democrat,* November 25, 1916.
19. *Kansas City Star,* September 24, 1916.
20. *St. Louis Globe-Democrat,* November 25, 1916.
21. *Kansas City Star,* September 24, 1916.
22. *St. Louis Globe-Democrat,* November 25, 1916.
23. Ibid., September 24, 1916.
24. "$3,450. Reward Circular for Ora Lewis, Frank Lewis, Oscar Lee."

CHAPTER 9: THE CAPTURE OF ORA LEWIS

1. *St. Louis Globe Democrat,* September 24, 1916.
2. Ibid., November 25, 1916.
3. Ibid., September 24, 1916.
4. Ibid, September 23, 1916.
5. *Kansas City Star,* September 23, 1916.
6. *St. Louis Globe-Democrat,* September 24, 1916.
7. Ibid.
8. Ibid.
9. Ibid.
10. Ibid.

11. Ibid.
12. Ibid.

CHAPTER 10: "WE ARE GOING TO BE POPPED"

1. *St. Louis Globe-Democrat,* November 29, 1916.
2. Ibid., November 16, 1916.
3. Ibid., November 21, 1916.
4. Ibid.
5. Ibid., November 25, 1916.
6. Ibid., November 26, 1916.
7. Ibid., November 27, 1916.
8. Ibid., November 28, 1916.
9. Ibid.
10. Ibid.
11. Ibid., November 30, 1916.
12. Missouri State prison records for Roy and Ora Lewis.
13. Donald Schroeger, "The Course of Corrections in Missouri, 1833-1983," in *Official Manual, Missouri, 1983–1984.* (Jefferson City: Office of Missouri Secretary of State, 1983), 1-23; "MSP Historical Information," *The Jefferson Journal, Historical ed.* (summer 1972).

CHAPTER 11: THE LEWIS-JONES GANG

1. Bailie, "Lewis Boys Gang."
2. Ibid.
3. *1900 Census*; *1910 Census*; Bailie, "Lewis Boys Gang."
4. Missouri state prison record of Roscoe Lancaster.
5. World War II draft registration of Roy Sherrill; *1910 Census*; United States Fidelity and Guaranty Company, *The True Story of the Last Crime and Capture of the "Lewis Gang"* (Baltimore, n.d.).
6. *Kansas City (MO) Times,* November 13, 1918.

7. Missouri state prison record of Thomas King.
8. *1910 Census*; Missouri state prison record of John Shead.

CHAPTER 12: THE CROSS-DRESSING BANDIT

1. *1900 Census*; *Los Angeles Times*, November 20, 1918; Missouri state prison record of Dale Jones.
2. Missouri state prison record of Dale Jones.
3. *Los Angeles Times*, November 20, 1918.
4. Ibid.
5. Ibid.
6. Ibid.
7. *Kansas City (MO) Times*, November 20. 1918.
8. *Kansas City Star*, November 23, 1913.
9. *Rich Hill (MO) Morning Review*, November 27, 1913.
10. Ibid., December 4, 1913.
11. Ibid.
12. Mattie Howard, *The Pathway of Mattie Howard (to and from Prison*, rev. ed. (New York: Pageant Press, 1963).
13. *Kansas City Star*, April 18, 1914; Watson, "Crimson Trail."
14. *Kansas City Star*, May 2, 11, 1914.
15. *Bates County (Butler, MO) Democrat*, June 11, 1914; *Butler (MO) Weekly Times*, June 11, 1914; *Chillicothe (MO) Constitution*, June 13, 1914.
16. Missouri state prison record of John Shead.

CHAPTER 13: "THE GIRL WITH THE AGATE EYES AND THE SMILE OF DEATH"

1. Howard, *The Pathway of Mattie Howard*, 76.
2. Howard, *The Pathway of Mattie Howard*; *1910 Census*.
3. *Atlanta Constitution*, March 27, 1921.
4. Howard, *The Pathway of Mattie Howard*.

5. *Atlanta Constitution,* May 27, 1921.
6. "$500 Reward for Mattie Howard," I. B. Walston, Chief of Detectives, Kansas City, MO, 1918.
7. Ibid.

CHAPTER 14: LOS ANGELES

1. Watson, "Crimson Trail." "The L. A. underworld was a chaotic jumble of competing families from the 1890s until nearly the end of the Prohibition Era." See "Crime Bosses of Los Angeles," *The American Mafia,* http://www.onewal.com/maf-b-la.html.
2. *Colorado Springs Evening Telegraph,* November 20, 1918.
3. *Kansas City (MO) Times,* November 20, 1918. In some accounts, Jones's benefactor was a man. See Watson, "Crimson Trail."
4. *Colorado Springs Evening Telegraph,* November 20, 1918.
5. *Los Angeles Times,* November 20, 1918.
6. Alan Hynd, "The Pinkertons and the Murdering Masquerader," *True Detective Mysteries,* July 1941; *1910 Census*; *Los Angeles Times,* November 20, 1918.
7. "Wanted Poster for Murder and Train Robbery—$2,000 Reward," Kansas City, MO, November 2, 1918.
8. *Indianapolis News,* January 20, 1923; letter to Mr. R. Dudley, New York City, January 27, 1942, Pinkerton Detective Agency files.
9. See Joliet prison records.
10. *Los Angeles Times,* November 21, 1918.
11. Ibid.
12. Ibid.
13. Ibid., November 20, 1918.
14. *Kansas City Times,* November 20, 1918.
15. Missouri state prison record of Dale Jones.
16. Bailie, "Lewis Boys Gang."
17. Watson, "Crimson Trail"; *Los Angeles Times,* November 21, 1918.
18. Watson, "Crimson Trail."
19. *Los Angeles Times,* December 9, 1917.

CHAPTER 15: MORE BANK ROBBERIES

1. *Denver Rocky Mountain News,* September 15, 1918; Bailie, "Lewis Boys Gang." Newspapers were searched for any reference to a bank robbery in Cement City, Kansas, but none were found. There is also a Cement City in Missouri. The Lewis-Jones gang was also reported to have robbed a bank in Chicago of $35,000 and killed a bank guard in 1918. No reference to this was found in the *Chicago Tribune.* See *Kansas City Star,* November 21, 1918, and *Los Angeles Times,* November 21, 1918, Moreover the gang may have robbed a bank in Bruceville, Indiana. See Murray, "The Lewis-Jones Gang."
2. *Kansas City Star,* February 4, 1918.
3. *Kansas City (MO) Times,* November 13, 1918.
4. *Kansas City (MO) Journal,* February 13, 1918.
5. Bailie, "Lewis Boys Gang"; Missouri state prison record of John Shead.
6. *Los Angeles Times,* November 21, 1918.
7. *Kansas City Star,* May 25, 1918.
8. Bailie, "Lewis Boys Gang."
9. Cliff Montgomery, "1918 'Spanish Flu'—Up to 40 Million Dead—A True Global Disaster," *SecretsofSurvival.com,* http://www.secretsofsurvival.com/survival/1918_spanish_flu.html.
10. Sarah Cummings, "Spanish Influenza Outbreak, 1918," International World History Project website, http://history-world.org/spanish_influenza_of_1918.htm.
11. Montgomery, 1918 'Spanish Flu.
12. Cummings, "Spanish Influenza."
13. Montgomery, 1918 'Spanish Flu.

CHAPTER 16: MURDER OF A DIAMOND KING

1. Watson, "Crimson Trail."
2. *Kansas City Star,* May 25, 1918.
3. Ibid., May 26, 1918.
4. Ibid., May 25, 1918.
5. Ibid., November 26, 1919.
6. Ibid., May 25, 1918.
7. Ibid., May 27, 1918.
8. Ibid., May 26, 1918.
9. Ibid., May 27, 1918.
10. "$500 reward for Mattie Howard."
11. *Kansas City Star,* May 27, 1918.
12. Ibid., May 26, 1918.
13. Ibid.
14. Ibid.
15. *Kansas City Star,* June 29, 30, 1918; "Crimes of the Sherrill-Lewis-Jones Gang," Pinkerton files.
16. *Kansas City Times,* November 13, 1918.

CHAPTER 17: TRAIN ROBBERY

1. Bailie, "Lewis Boys Gang"; *Kansas City (MO) Journal,* July 11, 1918.
2. *Kansas City Star,* July 17, 1918.
3. *Kansas City (MO) Journal,* July 11, 1918.
4. *Kansas City (MO) Star,* July 11, 1918.
5. Bailie, "Lewis Boys Gang"; *Kansas City (MO) Journal,* July 11, 1918.
6. *Kansas City (MO) Journal,* July 11, 1918.
7. Ibid.
8. Bailie, "Lewis Boys Gang"; *Kansas City Star,* July 11, 1918.
9. *Kansas City Star,* July 11, 1918.
10. Ibid.
11. *Kansas City Star,* July 17, 1918; Bailie, "Lewis Boys Gang."

12. *Kansas City Star,* July 17, 1918.
13. Ibid.
14. *Kansas City (MO) Times,* November 13, 1918.
15. Hynd, "Murdering Masquerader."

CHAPTER 18: DARING ESCAPES

1. *Kansas City Star,* July 20, 1918.
2. Bailie, "Lewis Boys Gang."
3. *Kansas City Star,* July 16, 1918.
4. Ibid., July 19, 1918.
5. Ibid., July 20, 1918,
6. Ibid., July 21, 1918.
7. "Kansas City LCN Family: The Balestrere Gang," ReoCities website, http://www.reocities.com/ocsmidwestmafia/kansascity.html.

CHAPTER 19: BANK ROBBERY IN INDIANAPOLIS

1. Hynd, "Murdering Masquerader"; *Indianapolis News,* August 8, 1918.
2. *Indianapolis News,* August 8, 1918.
3. Ibid.
4. Ibid.
5. Ibid.
6. Hynd, "Murdering Masquerader"; *Indianapolis News,* August 8, 9, 10, 1918.
7. *Indianapolis News,* August 8, 1918.
8. Hynd, "Murdering Masquerader."
9. *Indianapolis News,* August 13, 14, 1918; Hynd, "Murdering Masquerader."
10. Hynd, "Murdering Masquerader."
11. *Indianapolis News,* August 13, 1918.
12. Ibid., January 20, 1923.
13. Ibid., August 13, 1918.

CHAPTER 20: A TRIP TO DENVER

1. Hynd, "Murdering Masquerader."
2. Ibid. There were no radio cars at this time.
3. Ibid.
4. Ibid. The Marmon automobile was one of the premier vehicles of its time. It was the equal of the Pierce Arrow, Peerless, and Packard. The Marmon Wasp won the first Indianapolis 500 race of 1911. It was manufactured by Nordyke Marmon & Company of Indianapolis, Indiana, from 1902 through 1933. The 1916 Model 34 used aluminum in the body and chassis to reduce overall weight. A Model 34 was driven coast to coast as a publicity stunt, beating auto records. Marmon was famous for introducing the rearview mirror, as well as pioneering both the V16 engine and the use of aluminum in auto manufacturing. See the Marmon Club website, http://www.marmonclub.com/.
5. Hynd, "Murdering Masquerader."

CHAPTER 21: "THE WILDEST NIGHT"

1. Hynd, "Murdering Masquerader."
2. The Missouri state prison record of George Eudaley.
3. Hynd, "Murdering Masquerader."
4. *Colorado Springs Gazette,* September 14, 1918.
5. Ibid.
6. Ibid., September 19, 1918.
7. Ibid., September 14, 1918.
8. Hynd, "Murdering Masquerader."
9. *Colorado Springs Evening Telegraph,* September 16, 1918.
10. *Colorado Springs Gazette,* September 14, 1918.
11. *Colorado Springs Evening Telegraph,* September 19, 1918.
12. Ibid.
13. Ibid., September 16, 1918.

14. Ibid., September 19, 1918.
15. Ibid., September 14, 1918.
16. Colorado *Springs Gazette,* September 14, 1918.
17. Ibid.
18. Ibid.
19. *Colorado Springs Evening Telegraph,* September 25, 1918: *Kansas City Star,* September 25, 1918.,
20. *Colorado Springs Gazette,* September 25, 191
21. Ibid., September 14, 1918.

CHAPTER 22: MORE VIOLENCE

1. *Colorado Springs Gazette,* September 15, 1918.
2. *Denver Rocky Mountain News,* September 14, 1918.
3. *Colorado Springs Evening Telegraph,* September 17, 1918.
4. Watson, "Crimson Trail."
5. *Denver Rocky Mountain News,* September 14, 1918.
6. *Colorado Springs Evening Telegraph,* September 14, 1918.
7. Ibid.
8. Ibid.
9. Bailie, "Lewis Boys Gang."
10. *Colorado Springs Evening Telegraph,* September 14, 1918.
11. Bailie, "Lewis Boys Gang."
12. *Colorado Springs Gazette,* September 19, 1918.
13. IMDb, the Internet Movie Database website, http://www.imdb.com/.
14. *Denver Rocky Mountain News,* September 15, 1918.
15. *Colorado Springs Gazette,* September 14, 1918.
16. *Colorado Springs Evening Telegraph,* September 14, 1918.
17. *Colorado Springs Gazette,* September 14, 1918.
18. *Denver Rocky Mountain News,* September 15, 1918.
19. *Colorado Springs Evening Telegraph,* September 14, 1918.
20. *Colorado Springs Gazette*, September 14, 1918.
21. Ibid.
22. *Watson, "Crimson Trail."*
23. *Denver Rocky Mountain News,* September 15, 1918.

24. Ibid.
25. *Colorado Springs Evening Telegraph,* September 14, 1918.

CHAPTER 23: "THE MOST SPECTACULAR GUNFIGHT EVER WITNESSED IN THE CITY"

1. *Kansas City Star,* September 24, 25, 1918.
2. *Colorado Springs Evening Telegraph,* September 24, 1918.
3. Ibid., September 25, 1918.
4. Ibid.
5. Ibid.
6. *Tulsa Daily World,* September 25, 1918.
7. *Colorado Springs Evening Telegraph,* September 24, 1918.
8. Ibid., September 25, 1918.
9. Ibid. According to the *Kansas City Star* of September 24, 1918, two police officers chased two men in a speeding car to Roscoe Lancaster's hideout, which the officers entered after the two men went into the house. However, the following day the *Star* reported that the police officers went to the hideout after receiving a tip about Lancaster's location.
10. Ibid.
11. Ibid.
12. *Colorado Springs Evening Telegraph,* September 25, 1918; *Kansas City Star,* September 24, 1918.
13. *Colorado Springs Gazette,* September 25, 1918; *Colorado Springs Evening Telegraph,* September 25, 1918.
14. *Colorado Springs Gazette,* September 25, 1918.
15. Col*orado Springs Evening Telegraph,* September 25, 1918. "Blackie" lied about driving the Marmon. He was too seriously wounded to drive.
16. Hynd, "Murdering Masquerader."
17. *Colorado Springs Evening Telegraph,* October 3, 1918.
18. *Topeka (KS) Daily Capital,* October 17, 1918.
19. *Colorado Springs Gazette,* November 26, 1918.

CHAPTER 24: "YOUR LIFE IS IN GREAT DANGER"

1. Hynd, "Murdering Masquerader."
2. *Los Angeles Times,* October 30, 31, November 1, 1918.
3. *Kansas City (MO) Times,* May 25, 1918.
4. *Los Angeles Times,* November 1, 1918.

CHAPTER 25: "TWO BRIEF AND COLORFUL LIVES"

1. *Colorado Springs Evening Telegraph,* November 20, 1918.
2. *Los Angeles Times,* November 20, 1918.
3. *Colorado Springs Evening Telegraph,* November 20, 1918.
4. *Los Angeles Times,* November 20, 1918. Dean was at first thought to have killed Van Vliet, but later investigation found she could not have because he was at the back of the car, while she was in the front seat. See *Los Angeles Times,* November 22, 1918.
5. *Ibid.*, November 20, 21, 22, 1918.
6. Hynd, "Murdering Masquerader."
7. *Los Angeles Times,* November 26, 1918.
8. Lester Douglas Johnson, *The Devil's Front Porch* (Lawrence, KS: University Press of Kansas, 1970), 74.

CHAPTER 26: THE FALL OF MATTIE HOWARD

1. "The Girl with The Agate Eyes," *Atlanta Constitution,* March 27, 1921.
2. *Kansas City Star,* August 25, 1919.
3. "Agate Eyes."
4. *Kansas City Star,* October 26, 1919.
5. *Kansas City Star,* October 20, 1919; "Agate Eyes."
6. *Kansas City Star,* March 9, 1920; "Agate Eyes."

7. "Agate Eyes"; *Kansas City Star,* May 19, 1920.
8. *Kansas City Star,* November 16, 19, 1921; Missouri state prison record of Mattie Howard.

EPILOGUE

1. Missouri state prison record of Mattie Howard.
2. Howard, *Pathway of Mattie Howard.*
3. *Los Angeles Times,* January 15, 1970.
4. Missouri state prison record of Roy Joe Lewis.
5. *St. Louis Post-Dispatch,* January 7, 1941.
6. *Springfield (MO) Leader and Press,* August 4, 5, 6, 1972; Social Security Death Index of Roy Lewis..
7. Missouri state prison record of Ora Lewis.
8. *St. Louis Post-Dispatch,* June 13, 1920,
9. *Jefferson City (MO) Post Tribune,* April 24, 25, 1939.
10. Ibid., October 25, 30, 1939.
11. Missouri state prison record of Ora Lewis
12. Missouri Death Certificate 58-025978, Missouri State Archives online, http://www.sos.mo.gov/images/archives/deathcerts/1958/1958_00025978.PDF.
13. Leavenworth prison record of Roy Sherrill.
14. *Kansas City Times,* November 13, 1918.
15. Leavenworth prison record of Roy Sherrill.
16. *Indianapolis News,* July 5, 1921.
17. *Kansas City Times,* May 29, 1923; William J. Helmer and Rick Mattix, *The Complete Public Enemy Almanac* (Nashville, TN: Cumberland House, 2007), 145.
18. *Kansas City Times,* May 29, 1923.
19. Leavenworth prison record of Roy Sherrill; Atlanta penitentiary record of Roy Sherrill.
20. World War II draft registration record of Roy Sherrill.
21. Murray, "The Lewis-Jones Gang."
22. Missouri state prison record of John Shead.
23. Colorado state prison record of George Eudaley.

24. Leavenworth prison record of Thomas King.
25. Colorado state prison record of Eva Lewis.
26. *The Evening State Journal and Lincoln (NE) Daily News,* January 19, 1923.
27. Pinkerton report on Eva Lewis from A. H. Jones, superintendent of Kansas City, July 8, 1924, Sherrill-Lewis-Jones Gang, Pinkerton Detective Agency Files, Manuscript Division, Library of Congress.
28. Missouri death certificate 16305.
29. Bailie, "Lewis Boys Gang."
30. Helmer, *Public Enemy Almanac*, 334.
31. Bailie, "Lewis Boys Gang."

INDEX

www.ingramcontent.com/pod-product-compliance
Lightning Source LLC
Chambersburg PA
CBHW031512270326
41930CB00006B/369

* 9 7 8 0 6 1 5 6 6 0 4 2 4 *